MW01504670

SCHOLARS SPEAK!

A MOTIVATIONAL GUIDE TO
A MONUMENTAL MOUTHPIECE

The Money Of Public Speaking

CORY BRAZIER,
WILLIAM DOUGLAS
AND S. R. WILLIAMS I

Dedication

The Coach. The Mentor.

The etymologies of the following two words, coach and mentor, have multiple origins, which derive from the mid-18th century French, Hungarian, Latin, and Greek terms. The traced meanings can be closely associated with *the pulling along of closed cargo* (referencing the coach) and *guiding support to the less experienced* (referencing the mentor). This book, ***Scholars Speak: A Motivation Guide to A Monumental Mouthpiece; The Money Of Public Speaking,*** which stemmed from the work of both coach and mentor influence, is dedicated to the two roles that have been undervalued in the lives of so many.

We intend to highlight first the immeasurable impact of both, which are indispensable in a culture that lacks the practice of affirmations. *The Coach. The Mentor.* Without fanfare, subtly, they are the unsung champions of the public speaking world. You'll find them constantly motivating in the small rooms, the large rooms, one-on-one, or to the masses. The attitude that carries the idea that there's no room for rewarding these heroes will be silenced here. Mentorship is the face of polished accomplishment, paying it forward to the next goal-setter.

"Not creating them into your own image but giving them the opportunity to create themselves."

~ Steven Spielberg

A lifetime of coaching is what sparked a conversation between two brothers. One brother, coached by the other, returned the favor and planted the seed that led to a crop that harvested the start of a nonprofit organization that has grown into a mentoring ministry.

Shout out to all the Coaches and all the Mentors. We see you. ***Scholars Speak: A Motivation Guide To A Monumental Mouthpiece; The Money Of Public Speaking*** is dedicated to your example. Scholar Up!

Contents

Dedication i

Introduction iii

Chapter One: Gentlemen & Scholars Inc., The Substance And The Show 1

Chapter Two: SCHOLARS SPEAK! 5

Chapter Three: The Why-To Guide 10

Chapter Four: In The KNOW 15

Chapter Five: Key Principles 22

Chapter Six: A VOCALIZING WISE: Strategies, Fundamentals ... 31

Chapter Seven: Going Through the Fire BREEDS.................. 50

Chapter Eight: Innate To Engage 54

Chapter Nine: Body Has Dialect 60

Chapter Ten: Take Form & Scholar UP 72

Chapter Eleven: MONUMENTAL SPEECHES 79

Chapter Twelve: $tati$tical Pay $alarie$ 93

Chapter Thirteen: Marketing With Content Creation 110

Chapter Fourteen: Good Trouble 114

Chapter Fifteen: PROCRASTINATION 116

Chapter Sixteen: Short-Term, Long-Term................120

Chapter Seventeen: Underdog Stand Tall 122

Chapter Eighteen: Your Life Is Your Business...........124

Chapter Nineteen: Call-To-Action...........................131

Acknowledgments..135

About The Author 143

Sources 151

Introduction

Speak now or forever; hold your peace.

This guide is here to give you the motive to fulfill that ultimatum.

"Before we get started... is there anyone who wants to get out?"

This epic line will live on forever in the Marvel Cinematic Universe (MCU). In the movie *Captain America: Civil War (2016)*, those words were uttered by Steve Rogers—a spectacle of a soldier who stood as a symbol of never backing down—while being trapped, outnumbered, and surrounded by opposition, ready to attack him on a moving elevator. That line delivered just enough suspense needed to carry out every action sequence throughout the rest of the film.

So now let us say before we get started, just know that if you stay on, then you can do this. You can become this. The public speaker. The fact about public speaking, which is basically true of any pursuit of lasting impact, is that it can be done. We're here to tell you that you can do this, and there's an opportunity on the other side of these pages waiting for you or anyone you know with a little ambition. Such an opportunity bolds well for kids, especially.

It's not beyond the realm of possibility that the youngest voices have the most *mature-ish* durability for motivational acceptance. While looking for their way to attain what they deem as "motion," the youth possess a cutting-edge say-so as well, and it's our onus to bring it to the forefront. The money of public speaking is not only monetary, but it composes a number of works of merit.

We found out earlier on that you're either in the substance lane or the entertainment lane. We're here for 100 percent substance—but don't worry; we'll feature enough flash to uphold the pizzazz. While paying homage to the forefather of self-help literature, Dale Carnegie, author of The *Art of Public Speaking*, we're revealing that the golden age of this craft is right now. So, bring your ego because it's necessary.

Scholars Speak is not just another word salad. We're offering the language arts and disciplines of verbal mastery. When we commit to saying yes to ourselves, all spectators will watch the determination of a people, make a thriving business for their legacy. Say you will and become a stakeholder in your own established goals.

So let us ask again—before we get started, is there anyone who wants to get off this elevator? We will be going up and we already recognize the opposition.

Chapter One:
Gentlemen & Scholars Inc., The Substance And The Show

By design, the very name itself was chosen to be an odyssey that's meant to provoke an emotion that may excite action, a conversation piece. They stand for the respect of an upstanding identity, giving rise to the "getting power" of self-awareness.

You don't know it yet, but it's like a journey to the middle of the earth. The surface of their story, although entertaining enough, carries an undertone of relentless tenacity to win. To them, winning has a particular language. They call it *the Substance and the Show*.

Established in 2014 by William Douglas, Cory Brazier, and S. R. Williams I - *Gentlemen and Scholars Inc.* is a unique mentoring organization that travels abroad to educate all who are willing to obtain skillful speech. This objective is accomplished with the consistent onboarding of youth through their *Scholarship Spelling Bee Explosion* events coupled with their *School of Etiquette and Life Skills* classes. In addition, their speaking seminars have met many young and seasoned adults right where they're at, allowing them to be strengthened by a creed poised to a power of leadership and not popularity. *The Substance and the Show* philosophy will be outspoken as these Scholars Speak on the fundamentals. *Gentlemen and Scholars Inc....* it's an experience and a lifestyle.

A phrase like *"No one man has all the answers"* could be a thesis statement for those who seek to enlighten others. Therefore, it is against this backdrop that they would like to share their views about the career option of speaking professionally.

Individually and collectively as a team, all of them are exemplars of a formidable stage presence, which is their ethos. Each of them is highly decorated and accomplished in their own right with respect to delivering dynamic keynote addresses. They're the driving force behind a movement whose mission is to empower the youth and equip them with the tools necessary to become the best versions of themselves.

2

Furthermore, this is *us*—the merge of three distinguished approaches into one narrator. It is our vision to assist the thinkers of the future with unlocking their potential value, in order to maximize self-expression. Our organizational purpose is to provide an alternative to the mainstream and stereotypical path for young ladies and gents.

The majority of them have experienced so many situations that tell them the same story of feeling a sense of being held back in life. As the child reaches adulthood, the same feelings linger. One generation after another will accept that no matter what they pursue, it won't ring loud enough to give them a sense of being heard. A stellar education, talented sports achievements, and impressive financial accomplishments can still fall short of fulfilling our inner voids of a muted language.

We ask ourselves in the silence of our souls why we struggle to find our voice. Some have found it and wish to perfect it, while others are afraid to look, sunk in the quicksand of fear.

Even though *Gentlemen and Scholars Inc.* has accepted the calling to help mitigate the wayward decisions of a child, they have also embraced the role of influencers and have been led to mentor the progress of people at every stage of life.

Mindset mentoring is actually their life's work. There is no business that doesn't require a vocal visionary whose task is to spread the message that points in the direction of profit and, or impact. The business model that takes shape and thrives is the one that has a sum of all the parts, believes in, and embodies the philosophy of the company.

Some of us are born to do it, and others are trained into it, but there's not one clear path to becoming a savant, and unfortunately, it's not even that absolute. Some will even remain silent until the very end, and yet we pass no judgment. There's a time and place to use your Miranda rights, but in this fleeting hour of affirming dreams to life, we wouldn't advise it.

"There is no greater agony than bearing an untold story inside you."

~Maya Angelou

Chapter Two:
SCHOLARS SPEAK!

Scholars Speak! is a motivational guide to a monumental mouthpiece.

First things first: let's address the desired outcome for the readers of this speaker's playbook. No matter your age, race, profession, or social status, this guide will provide impactful insight into the wonderful world of oration.

Motivation and discipline both have their place in our lives, but nothing can substitute for taking action. This book serves as an intermediary bridge between all three components—a liaison for countless souls whose time has come to speak truth to power.

By granting ourselves liberty while stranded in uncertainty, you'll discover that the mind presents more of an impediment than the tongue. From birth, we instantly know *courage*, as it comes with curiosity. However, time itself presents an inescapable amnesia, making us less familiar with the bravery needed to proclaim openly. Now, all we remember is the fear of judgment.

Even a victim of the *glossophobia* condition, which is the fear of public speaking and affects up to 75% of the population, has a fair chance to step into their firmness of mind and profess with confidence what they know to be of substance.

There stands in leadership an essential constituent of the human appetite for recognition, a force that carries universal cachet, dominion and rule in its purest form. This hunger to be heard by the masses sits dormant within all of us, waiting for permission to be awakened, and manifests itself in other ways if ever repressed for too long.

Children have an innate knowledge that there must be a way to cry out to everyone for what they want. Imagine waiting a lifetime and finally learning how to release your voice effectively and why to become skillful at it. This is a moment for all of posterity, beginning with a generation's call for highlighting one of the five freedoms placed in the Constitution. Freedom of speech, for which there is no substitute, allows individuals to address issues verbally and without interference, standing at a podium with a sense of pride.

So, it's due time to live by this philosophy that you shall become a scholar in the scope of work that you deem worthy of gaining understanding. When you can share your experiences and wisdom on the big stage with a great host of people—stirring up emotion and promoting the better way—clarity tends to seek you out and rest with you.

A word spoken in front of a crowd is reinforced by those who are thoughtful before speaking. It'll give solace to utterance, like a much-needed cheer for voice rehabilitation. So, in this case, speech becomes therapy.

The highest form of self-expression is the truest example of the Creator's formulating statement of *"Let there be light."*

We want to extend acclaim to the industry that has developed the mindset and reputation of so many prolific thought leaders of today: the industry of public speaking. This performance term is often defined as *the act or process of organizing prepared speeches in public.* What's presented is intentional, purposeful and traditionally meant for speaking in person to a live audience. Yes, public speaking is the opportunity to occupy various platforms that make you relatable enough to win over countless crowds while informing, entertaining, and persuading with a language of momentum.

Interestingly enough, this industry is unique because it has a very low barrier to entry yet ranks remarkably high in its professional return. Which is significant to mention because this skill is like a diamond that's close to the average grasp but elusive to the touch of many.

If implemented properly and consistently, Scholars Speak principles will start a transformational process that leads to being an effective yet polarizing communicator. We want you to accomplish that level of confidence within yourself that will resonate like sound doctrine to others.

We're in the genesis stage of this guide, but we're still encouraging a call to action. We want to propose that you consider enrolling in our *Scholars Speak Agency and Course.*

This book is a mentorship rendition of our coaching community support, which is a hands-on, day-to-day journey of becoming a professional speaker. The one who understands the laws of unity by voice understands that any form of censorship

should never be self-inflicted. So, speak now or forever, hold your peace and Scholar Up!

Chapter Three:
The Why-To Guide

Discovering the Wealth of Self-Expression

Usually, when someone chooses to read a book of this nature, they have their initial expectations. Yes, in some respects, it holds plenty of how-to's for public speaking purposes, but above all, it's more of a *why-to* guide. In other words, it's in the "wherefore" that it must begin. Whether they are drawn by the appeal to be motivated, to be inspired, or to gain some sort of knowledge, the same is expected for this book, and we wouldn't have it any other way.

Expectations play a major part in getting lasting results because you have to assume from the very beginning that there's something valuable for you to keep moving forward in that direction. The direction of mastering the power of your voice can certainly bring you all the things your heart desires.

It is said, *"Ask and you shall receive,"* but the skillful ability to ask comes from confidence in speaking your truth. William Shakespeare said, *"The world is a stage,"* so you can play along with their program or speak up for yours.

Make no mistake, we are the ones we've been waiting for.

~Things to Expect

Yes, motivation, yes, inspiration, and yes, knowledge. But not just those.

Scholars Speak will help you see your purpose before you execute it. There is a chance that standing on a platform with hundreds of people listening to you may or may not happen for you. Yet, standing in your confidence with the inner tools to make an unforgettable statement in front of any crowd could happen today!

By no means are we claiming to be the leading authority on the subject of public speaking. However, we *are* claiming that this book can be your go-to resource of all resources in understanding the power and authority of your voice. There are plenty of people who decided to embark on this path, and after committing the hours required on this journey are now making all their dreams come true.

And yet, others decided to start in this industry who didn't reap the results they desired and quit. With anything, if you do it well enough, there'll be plenty of money in it. The money will always come because it follows the proper activity, which leads to productivity and will only come and be sustained with the right philosophy and attitude. With this mindset, there's always a chance to succeed, and without it an equal chance of failure. But even with that said, failure loses its sting if you don't quit.

We encourage you to give yourself a chance and start molding yourself into your very own public spokesman or woman or person.

Like the words of *Gentlemen and Scholars'* executive advisor, **C. Shawn Thomas,**

"Progress, not perfection."

~Your Permissive Will

Scholars Speak is a book that will give permission. Permission to what, you say? Permission to unlock fear prisons.

It will open up and release an imprisoned person that you consider naturally happy but who's actually hidden and trapped. But truly, that trapped person has the voice of freedom that defines your legacy.

In the study of physics, sound is a vibration that propagates as an acoustic wave through a transmission medium such as a gas, liquid, or solid. In human physiology and psychology, sound is the reception of such waves and their perception by the brain.

Simply put, despite the complex process and its workings, the human voice and the ability to communicate our thoughts with words and sounds is one of the things that makes us unique from animals. But our guess is most people don't understand or simply don't care about the power of their voice, especially not for the sake of sharing it in front of a large audience of people. But they may fail to realize that public speaking in and of itself is not for the purpose of showing off popularity, being idolized, or the stroking of one's ego.

Public speaking is a very misunderstood skill and probably the most exciting form of self-expression. It allows us to form connections, influence decisions, and motivate change. Without communication skills, the ability to progress in the ever-moving world and in life itself would be nearly impossible.

What's probably misunderstood the most is the rationale behind speaking face-to-face to a live audience. The term can quickly send one into a frenzy of overwhelming fear just by envisioning a sea of faces staring at them as they begin to articulate an idea or a thought that they thought they knew well.

In today's times, we've all seen countless video clips of a prominent influencer, motivational speaker, actor, rapper, film star, or celebrity charismatically performing a dialog in front of a large gathering as they respond with a standing ovation. We may think to ourselves, *"No wonder they're famous. I could never see myself up there, and yet I would love to be able to do that and think, how can that ever come to be?"*

Others might think that *"such reality could never be for me because I could never be that person."* The art of public speaking can actually transcend the stereotypical performer into the image of powerful leadership. Just by definition, even a school teacher, student council presenter, politician, and comedian are all public speakers.

Public speaking has been called one of the most important skills known to mankind. It will give you an incredible professional advantage. What lies within us is more than data; it's *life.* How that life comes out of us could be the difference in our successes and failures.

Chapter Four:
In The KNOW

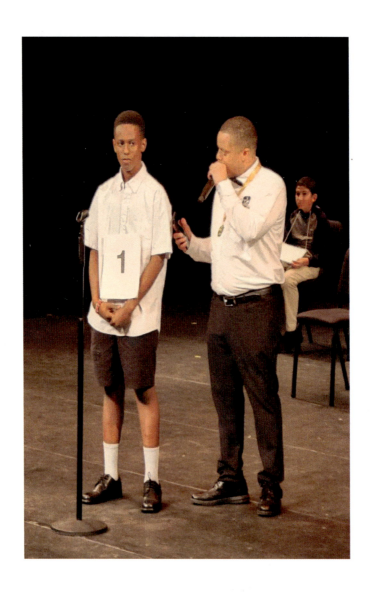

~Know The Benefactor

Try approaching all your speaking appearances in the spirit benevolence, simply to give and offer up and not just to take for gain. Although gaining has its place, evidently, conventional wisdom agrees that greatness is achieved in the service to many. If you're not careful, you can miss a valuable lesson in the giver vs. taker mentalities.

Give it all. Coming in with the mind to give is what sets apart the all-but-typical clever talk for the passing of time from an ever-so impactful life-changing call-to-action. These types of intentions are premeditated. Planning to give of yourself and laying it all on the line for the sake of enhancing someone's well-being is a living sacrifice felt by the receiving hand. It won't be taken for granted but appreciated in so many moments before they start to applaud you.

The universal law of reciprocity will show itself true when you least expect it. Show up with a giving attitude. You know something, and you can't keep it for yourself. Share the life. You've seen something you can't hide and must describe it. Share the life because you want your audience to live better than you. So, give it all, and they'll surely come back.

Or option number two—take it all. Coming in with the mind to take says you were never complete from the start. There will be something to gain from every opportunity you have to speak, but the timing of reaching for it must be done with acute discretion. The what's-in-it-for-me energy can be sensed even when value is being provided. You're projecting that you are needy and unfilled, which is the image that repels an audience's attention.

If you're serious about going the professional path at some point, you must understand that your eagerness to take the spoils may leave you with a never-again-to-return audience. Some purposeful advice for walking in with the right mindset; now, you can take it or leave it.

"Courage is what it takes to stand up
and speak and sit down and listen."

~ **Winston Churchhill**

~Know Yourself

We live in an era of social media filters and trend-setting influencers, where identity crises are running rampant, and television imagery is programming the definition of what's acceptable and exceptional. We are so busy trying to become someone who is something to all people instead of being who we are for ourselves. It gets even worse when low self-esteem is the driving force behind this urge.

Even though the dangers of sun gazing have likely been well documented, yet the dangers of "stargazing" have gone unchecked. You can't help but want to be like, speak like, or act like the celebrity or movie star you see on the screen. All too often, we fall into idolizing people who we don't know and wouldn't even care to know us. Being content with who you are has become a lost art. We're constantly comparing ourselves with an unattainable idea of appeal.

Comparisons often lead to a lack of personal inner peace. This so-called appeal you seek will cause a repelling effect; you'll see people withdrawn, leaving you wondering and thinking to yourself, *"I don't get it... was it something I said?"* So, it's truly an understatement when we say authenticity engages audiences, so use the *you* factor to bridge the gap when speaking. Imitating someone else's style might allow you to get into more than a few rooms, but your power will come when you embrace what makes you unique.

You can't be someone else and make a real name for yourself. So, if you're not them and you're not acting like you, then you're *nobody* up there on stage talking. Establishing a comfortable sense of self without inner judgment will develop the confidence needed to address any crowd.

But first, you have to know yourself, which includes your standards, expectations, morals, desires, and purpose. Before you address an audience, why not ask yourself, "Who am I right now?"

Believe us when we say it'll matter because they can feel realness.

~ Know the Surroundings

Awareness connects you to the audience. Situation awareness: sometimes, things will not go as planned.

From a collection of memorable quotes, our fan-favorite regarding this book is *"to sway an audience; you must watch them as you speak"* by *Nectar, in a Nutshell* author **C. Kent Wright**.

Unless you've mastered the skill of forecasting unlikely events, it's safe to say the unpredictable is bound to happen while you're delivering your speech. These events can be categorized as *mini, minor,* or *major.* You must be aware of your surroundings so you can connect with your audience immediately.

The key is to establish what basketball savvy calls *the home court advantage.* One rule of engagement states that you have to see who's approaching first, so you can open the door before they knock; welcome them in, and your surroundings will never see you coming. The auditorium is filling up, and everyone's energy is registering to you; it is the measuring stick you'll learn to read quickly before you even start. Each audience section will take on its personality and you can precede on knowing how to interact with them, even with a rehearsed speech. Knowing your surroundings, a skill that requires the time and the reps to enlarge your discerning territory.

"It's alright to have butterflies in your stomach;

just get them to fly in formation."

~ Rob Gilbert

~Know Audacity

Shock value is what we want to leave the room with as often as possible. Moments when people just can't believe what we said should happen periodically. Dare to be controversial while being selective of what informs and inspires. You have to be bold in order to deliver something informative. We won't allow them to get away from us, thinking that what we gave them was boring and lacked courage.

Sometimes, you have to step out of yourself and be the surprise that intimidated the old you. You have to be outgoing to deliver something that is taboo to the ears. You have to be unpredictable to deliver something inspiring. You have to catch a few people off guard from time to time and keep them guessing so they can take you seriously. Gamble a little bit and play the odds with what you say to yourself first and then what you relay to your listener.

For example, dare to recite affirmations every day that declares, *"I'm so happy now that I am one of the most influential public speakers, and everyone loves my energy and wants to invite me back."* Or *"I am one of the best and most requested presenters, so people all over love paying me top dollar for my speeches."*

Thinking this way might allow you to also start speaking this way. The habit of walking in your audacity as a natural state magnifies the lure that sits in your aura. This attraction factor will be felt by all who enter the same room as you. Indeed, people notice, so you literally become the life of the party. Take a chance in actually going against the restraint of being normal. Know the audacity within you and free it.

Chapter Five:
Key Principles

Essence of Perception

Cease striving to be a great public speaker. Instead, become comfortable with the speaker you will become. Which includes constantly reaching for the best version of yourself.

Suppose public speaking is the craft of effective oral communication with an audience. Doesn't that also apply to what any individual at a simple dinner outing does on any given normal occasion anyway? Yes, it even applies to a silly karaoke gathering amongst friends with no pressure to perform at all.

Where does it say that you have to be standing or that you have to be delivering a speech on wide-ranging topics of world innovation? All it says is that you have to have effective oral communication with an audience. We all love listening to someone interesting, relaxed, and comfortable because they make us feel safe and unguarded in the moment.

We have no problem being ourselves in daily conversations and interactions. Yet, too often, when we stand up to give a speech, something changes. We all too often focus on the public at the expense of the speaking. In all actuality, just the opposite must be done: focus on the speaking and let the public go.

Here are some tips to do just that:

The Perfect Illusion

Even the most decorated speaker will make a mistake or two at some point. Just keep in mind that you'll likely be the one to notice more than anyone who's a part of your audience.

One of the most important things you can do after making a mistake during a presentation is to keep going. Don't stop—unless the blunder was truly devastating—never apologize to the audience for a minor slip-up. If they don't have a copy of your speech as you're delivering it, the audience won't be aware of the fact that you left out a word, referenced the wrong name, or even skipped a paragraph. To quote Alexander Pope, *"To err is human;"* a mistake can actually assist you in some cases because it allows your listeners to relate to you in the space of interesting imperfection. People don't want to hear someone *perfect* but rather passionate; they will connect much more easily to the person who shows to be real.

Master the dexterity of public speaking, and you'll absolutely conquer your next speech delivery. So just keep reading to *Scholar Up!* You're almost there.

The Creative Visualization Skillset

High achievers in all aspects of life have at least one thing in common. They practice visualization to achieve their goals; whether they knew it or not, it certainly worked for them.

People of business envision themselves making successful deals, corporate officials have pictured themselves developing the next big venture, and even athletes imagine themselves breaking records while pushing their bodies to the limit as they perform another exciting feat that amazes the crowd. They all see it in their mind's eye first.

The same is true in the space of public speaking. We all know about the feeling of butterflies in the stomach—the nervousness. It's natural to have a sense of anxiety when getting ready to step in front of people.

A great way to resolve nervousness and become a more comfortable speaker is to rehearse in the one place where no one can see you—in your mind. If you visualize regularly and see it before it happens, you'll prepare your state of mind for future opportunities to speak in public while conquering the infamous butterflies.

Many of us have a great fear of speaking in public only because we don't do it that often. Reprogram your mind. To program a system is to instill in it the tools it needs to be productive.

The mind is a system with lingering hindrances. We must make it our habit to imagine ourselves confidently speaking to become used to it. You must be willing to train your mind to focus on it. You must put in the mind work and the mind practice to believe that it is natural to speak proudly and this is all a very comfortable environment. It is all-important that you see yourself in front of the room, see yourself there, then stand in front of the room, and then command it to be a true sight come to life.

A Discipline Mind

There is no such thing as a *perfect* public speaker. What you should aim to be is an *impactful* speaker. This type of impact simply means to affect someone's life through perspective by introducing purposeful action. Like anything else in life, it takes practice not just to improve those speaking skills, but also to enhance them.

We take communication for granted all too often because we speak to people daily. Whether it be in your home with family, at work on the job, or just amongst your peers in a recreational setting. See, when your success is directly connected to how well you perform in front of a group, it's a must that you give the task the same attention as if you were a professional athlete. Yes, the discipline it takes to train the body is also required when training the voice. It also speaks to the strength of your focus. It stands in the case of all things progressive. Discipline is what adds power to the process.

Remember, even world champion athletes practice and practice and practice every day.

Being Personally Descriptive

The key to effective oration is to make it personal. The bottom line is that it's your testimony; no matter what topic, audiences respond best when the presenter can make their message hit home to the soul. Think of it as a conversation between you and the audience. If you can carry on a fluid conversation with two or more people, you can give a great speech.

Whether your audience consists of two people or two thousand and whether you're talking about the latest life achievement or what you did today at work, be yourself, talk directly to people and make a memorable connection with them. What's from the heart reaches the heart, as we all know. It's a terrific way to get intimate with large audiences. Use every opportunity to use your emotions to put a face on the facts of your presentation.

Most people love to hear about other people's stories—the victories, the heartbreak, and even the everyday humor that serves as a much-needed recipe to fulfill their life's appetite. Telling stories will give you the type of credibility that draws in the most skeptical thinkers and yet helps them become the listeners you seek to engage. As much as possible, make a conscious effort to add a personal interest element to your speaking engagements. Your listeners will warm up to you the more you utilize this technique, and it will also be therapeutic for you as it puts you at ease by assisting you in overcoming any residual nervousness. Simply put, what are you more of an expert in than in the subject of yourself?

Who Is Your Listener?

Roll call is checking with the members of the group to establish who's present by reading their names. Headcounts are not likely to happen in a stadium full of people. You still must know who the listener is who stands before you. Some have come to see you prevail, and others come to watch you fail.

Being cognizant of exactly what type of audience you're in front of is crucial when it comes to occupying stages. Having an idea of the genre of the listener you're speaking to allows you to customize your dialog in a way that will be most engaging for them. It helps you anticipate the questions and concerns they may have and embrace those in your presentation. It also allows you to use resonating language and examples that your audience will best relate to for an easier understanding of the message you are delivering.

Be sure to do your research ahead of time so you do not have to ever go into any presentation blindly. Whether it be an audience of ten or ten thousand, it'll be very helpful for you if you know the background of the location. Get familiar with the cultural practices of the area so you know what to incorporate during your introduction segment. For instance, when speaking in a university setting, you can always use references of their past alumni in your presentation. Using historical achievements and interesting facts pertaining to the city or town you're speaking in simply tells them that you have made the extra effort to dig a little deeper to connect with them.

Not only will they appreciate the mentionable inclusions, but they will certainly remember your presentation as if it were a cherished conversation with a friend.

The Goal of Leaving Them Wanting More

One of the most valuable lessons learned from our years of training others on how to communicate is that when it comes to the essence of public speaking, less is usually more and usually enough. We've never witnessed, within any speaker's setting, someone say " I wish that this speech was longer." However, we can assume how many times they've thought, *"This speech is taking forever. I'm so glad it's over."*

So, shock your audience from time to time. Make your presentation just a tad shorter than they anticipated. If you take into consideration the principle of supply and demand, it's better to leave your listeners always wanting more. In other words, keep them on the edge of their seats to the very end.

~Stage Presence

"The energy level of the audience is the same as the speakers, for better or for worse."

~ Andras Baneth

"It was a vibe."

It's what we hear people say nowadays when they're at a gathering, and the mood of it flows and gives life to the attendees. The vibe or vibration they speak of is the energetic frequency of the electromagnetic field (the aura) of the people. We all have a vibe; sometimes its signature ranges high, and sometimes it's low, but it's always resonating.

It's no secret that most people want to be around energy that contributes to their well-being and flee from what is draining. Even on a stage, your energy will mark its territory across an entire area.

Whether it's yelling genius or defeatist, it's communicating loud. So why not prepare your mood to win? Your mood is a colorful outfit you put on daily, and you have to monitor that fashion statement you're trying to make.

There's no shortage of ways to raise your vibration, just start with how to improve your overall health in general, and it'll overlap in the total fullness of you. One's vitality is prevalent with stage presence, which is an indicator of how you walk in your confidence. Even recognizing this from a business angle, your ability to be a mature and literally monumental presence on stage can command your righteous payday.

You'll find out very quickly that the stage effect has an immediate and powerful financial return. Even while off-stage, your stage presence holds true. It helps you sell things better; it helps you get the job you want; it helps you to get that promotion; it helps you get the funding for your business; and it helps you recruit people for your company. It is the ability to leverage something that makes it very powerful. In order for it to work, though, you have to have some skills, but most importantly, you have to be wearing the mood of an unprecedented giant. Now crush it, but be careful where you step because even a titan has a weakness that keeps them humble before they exit stage left.

Chapter Six:
A VOCALIZING WISE: Strategies, Fundamentals

The Ingenuity in the Pause: 3-5-second rule:

You've already been introduced, you've walked on stage, and they, the crowd, haven't really settled down to listen yet. For whatever reason, the proper mood wasn't set for them to feed off your words.

What do you do? Nothing. Not yet. Just wait, look, and do nothing. Always start your speech with a 3-to-5-second moment of silence. What this pause does is give your audience a moment to settle in and pay attention to your presentation. The attention you seek is undivided, so implementing the pause increases the odds of drawing in wandering minds.

~ The pause. The pause does wonders for both the speaker and the listener because it allows us to be slightly present with our feelings as if they're seeds, sinking anchors into the soil right before taking root. But it's truly the after-effect of the pause that catches spectators by surprise and is the greatest first impression widely known as captive. Yet there will come a time when the moment feels too big for the speaker, inviting an uneasiness that grips and apprehends the confidence. This hijacking of one's boldness is unplanned, of course, but daunting nonetheless.

So, a preemptive approach must be taken to establish the rule of composure to at least appear unshaken. For the speaker who makes use of slowing down and stopping before they begin, this habit can serve as a therapeutic elixir to remedy the affliction of nervousness. It has a way of calming the anxious butterflies and resetting the aim of the trembling bow and arrow that's ready for release—an excellent opportunity to step into your inner Robin Hood. Now, for the listener, it awakens their natural inclination to notice the silence, which triggers a leaning-in reaction as if to eavesdrop on a secret.

Dead Air

Starting your speech with a pause allows for an early introduction of suspense, a build-up to the crescendo before one word is even spoken. Pauses can also be of benefit when applied throughout the duration of the speech as well. These uncommunicative interludes can serve as great replacements for filler words like *"uh," "um," "ah,"* and other repetitive phrases that are tell-tell signs the speaker has drawn a blank while attempting to find a word to express the next idea.

What makes the power of spoken words so impactful is the empty space, otherwise known as the *'dead air'* between each one of them. Likened to the sequence of a waltz, the music halts, and the hush takes the dance floor, in stillness it commands all respect until it has your commitment, then reaches for and grabs the hand of the voice and proceeds to glide as the music resumes—a peaceful oxymoron that rhythmically penetrates the ears. Every time you pause, you're allowing the audience time to think about what you have said. The art of being non-verbal is a survival technique, a way to ration the attention span, for one to process your message as if it carries its own autocorrect function, perfectly spacing and placing a moment for punctuation as your voice sustains its pledge.

"Inhale the Future, Exhale the Past."

Let It Breathe...

To even attempt to speak life into someone's being begins with the component most taken for granted—the breath. The evidence of an ever-existing presence felt an invisible river current moving through our insides. There's no life without breathing. Just because this process is involuntary doesn't mean you shouldn't intentionally work at it like any other skill. The study and mastery of breath work could be the single most important practice anyone could involve themselves in, not just to be used to perform under duress but for the clear purposes of an ultimate state of well-being. Poor mental health has been uncovered as a growing issue that has been ignored and not taken seriously in this modern, fast-paced society. Life is happening all too well, so anxiety can prove to be a real problem at the absolute wrong time.

Proper breathing is crucial for effective public speaking, especially if you're prone to rushing through your talk. For some reason, the average person tends to hold their breath at the height of any intense moment. This habit can be even tumbling the sharpest, and most conditioned individuals in every walk of life, including sports.

Believe it or not, it even happens in the beginning stages of boxing while training. The novice that puts on the gloves and starts to wail away often finds themselves out of breath within seconds just after a few punches in. Due to his eagerness, he who is untrained is unaware of their lack of self-discipline to pace. The unskillful boxer and inept speaker both will fall victim to situations that become inconsequentially breathtaking.

Take into consideration that whenever the mind lacks focus, it is overcrowded with an assortment of attention-pulling thoughts. No matter how insignificant, those inner voices will call for your regard. While debating for your reaction, the involuntary head talk argues amongst itself its point of view, all at once, alongside every mental depiction imitating popcorn by hopping up and down. The inner talk blares so loud that it can create an overwhelming, suffocating effect that's displayed outwardly—a perfect place for a pause, as discussed above. *Now,* take a moment for yourself and breathe.

Breathing as we know it to be is supposed to be easy because it's what we do without thinking every second in life. But the calculated breath that is on purpose and intentional can be what invites the transformative. Found in the core principles of some religious practices are the ideas that relate the breath to the very spirit of man. Whether it be accurate/conclusive or not, can't be determined, but the concept is that these terms are connected, and *'breath'* can be translated to mean *'spirit.'* This statement is only relevant to express that, in a sense, taking a series of deep breaths can be the beginning of a spiritual awakening. That calculated breath can lead to an *'aha!'* moment of enlightenment right before or in the midst of a pressured-filled speech. Take deep breaths from the diaphragm to support your voice and control your nervousness.

Turn Up the Volume!!!

Through our signature program, *the School of Etiquette and Life Skills, Gentlemen and Scholars Inc.,* as an organization, we teach the youth that their voice is their superpower. For this reason our instructors begin each class with the volume of their voices turned all the way up to the number ten dial. Then, we ask our audience why they think we do so.

You would think while in the classroom that the person teaching aims to avoid any vocal amplifying is doing so for the sake of keeping everyone's inside energy calm. But we promote the exact opposite in most cases. Therefore, we must note that when teaching the concepts of superpowers to us, they are defined as very achievable abilities that are beyond humans and nature. Two words, when put together, describe one's entailing capabilities that are paranormal and extraordinary. Powers so diverse in their expression, these potentialities are certainly all-encompassing from the mundane to the almighty, and so there is no limit to what superpowers are.

We hammer home this point because what lies within everyone of us is the most interesting noise that carries a signature purpose but yet is still subject to be muted or even turned off. With that said, there comes a time when you must know that you can't be boxed in no matter what rules are declared, and in that time, you must exercise your special talent.

We've challenged many soft-spoken individuals to listen to themselves shout their truth. Every person has the capacity to raise their confidence in any setting. In certain cultures, we've learned to appreciate the privilege of just being able to make any type of loud sound.

Even as children coming up, we were told in so many ways to never talk back, and in some respects, we should only be seen and not heard. It's funny because phrases like *"shut up," "shush,"* and *"shhh"* were a common part of our English development. Now, understanding somewhat of how the young mind works, being told such things so early in age allows for the subconscious to take hold and promote the growth of a message not conducive to self-expression.

So, you should try your best to speak loudly enough to be heard by everyone in the room, especially in the back, and to do it without shouting. Vary your volume to emphasize important points and keep your audience engaged. Strangely enough, two things can be true to the fact, meaning sometimes a whisper is needed. Even this very point needs to be expounded upon. Not to sound condescending of the prior claims that were just made for raising your voice but the art of the undertone holds plenty of weight in this discussion as well.

In the midst of any speech, your volume literally takes on its own personality and draws its own patronage. From the whisper, people will lean in just to feel like they are the special guests who were invited to the soirée and must RSVP. Through repetition, you'll gain experience in learning how to discern the right time to harness these elements of volume and their power over them.

Pitch Perfecto

The late great Christopher Reeves was best known for playing the role of the Man of Steel in the 1980s classic *Superman*. He delivered a spectacular performance by not only making himself believable and capturing the iconic posture of the heroic character traits of Superman but also portraying the undesired personality of his less impressive alter ego, Clark Kent. Like most things, the details can be lost or go unnoticed in the height of action.

In this historical motion picture, whenever Superman talked, his voice carried an energy with strength behind it, meant to be taken with all seriousness, a force of life and death. Usually, after every eye-catching feat, the day was saved, and his mediocrity was cued back in. As normalcy would have it Superman would elect to return to his shell to become Clark again. Along with a simple change of outfit and glasses, he purposely raises the octave when he speaks, which unconsciously causes his peers to perceive him as weaker and unworthy and so they ignore him.

What's fascinating about him is that he knew that by slightly adjusting his voice, the nature of the human psyche could be manipulated into an imminent response. It's humorous in the fact that they would look right at him in the face and only see a disguise because he spoke softer and higher. You don't have to fly to prove your words have the power to reach the sky. Yet this might be the closest you get to seeing through walls—the walls of people's cognizance. You have this said ability. The way to sway one's perception of you is certainly found in how equipped you are by learning to maneuver your mouthpiece.

Apart from the public speaking arena we must remember that we are having a conversation with our listener. It doesn't always have to be looked at as a performance. Everyone wants a chance to convey their idea and, or feeling within that very moment of expression. This desire makes us relatable and thus attractive to the company we keep and the ones who choose to hear us out. The more natural we are while speaking, the more trustworthy we're perceived to be.

People who listen to us are looking for reasons to trust us and searching for evidence through our acute tendencies that reveal who we really are. It's said that people must like you, know you, and trust you before they'll buy into you or your idea. Explaining the liking and knowing elements of connection can be for another time. However, what you might not know is that the trust element is found in our pitch.

The human voice serves as an important prediction source of social knowledge and attractive qualities that correlate to withdrawal and repel. The perfect pitch, a commonly used term, truly is only ever determined by the one who seeks their own definition of an auditory sensation. Simply meaning it matters even to the one who cares not to listen yet can't help but tune in because attraction is not a choice. Just ask the pick-up artist at your local cocktail lounge.

You can get what you want from almost anybody if you learn to speak their language. At the very least, you'll have their ear. Though there are many ways to execute strategies related to this, we must remind you this is a why-to book and these are why-to concepts. You should consider practicing modifying your tone in hopes of dedicating the change to a specific part of your speech to add a spark that jolts a longer attention span.

Male or female voice frequency patterns are a perceptual property of sounds governed by the rate of vibrations producing them. All can be imitated to a degree of highness or lowness of a tone. Even the psychology behind it states that people with lower frequency voices tend to view themselves as others do to be relatively more confident, strong, and authoritative than people with higher pitch voices. To be fair, a word spoken with a higher pitch injected at the right time of a speech can hijack the attention of any listener. This is where humor is best inserted or even sustained for entertainment purposes.

The diverse use of your pitch can keep your audience engaged in so many subtle ways. Nonetheless even this simple task can pose a challenge if you're not seasoned in the techniques of pitch adjustment. It's also to be noted that something as undetectable as the social status of the listener can alter our voice. Studies have found that unconsciously, people tend to change the pitch of their voice depending on who they are talking to and how dominant they feel. So, speak with excitement as if you realize that every sound that leaves your mouth represents a note from every piano key struck. Master this, and it'll be music to the ears. However, regardless of this concert and arrangement of words, audiences will trust and respond to speakers who are passionate about their subject matter. Be passionate, and remember that trust is found in the pitch.

Articulation:

The Key to Communication

It's ironic how what you hear affects what you see. Your appearance in the eyes of others will often be determined by how clearly you're understood. Articulation is the overall result of speech components working together in harmony. If you're going to speak, it's to your benefit, and everyone else's, that you deliver your message in such a way that you are viewed as competent.

Everybody uses articulation every day. Without articulation, it would be difficult to understand what someone is saying to you, and conversation can be misinterpreted. If someone has difficulty with the articulation of certain sounds, the meaning of their sentence may change because of the way they say certain words. Articulation, therefore, makes it easier for everyone to understand what is being said, and it makes the conversation clear and easy to understand.

Enunciate your words so that everyone in the audience can understand you. Use correct pronunciation to ensure that you pronounce words correctly to avoid misunderstandings.

Mr. William Douglas expressed that while taking his first public speaking course at a local college, he realized that he was actually the walking personification of what the class set out to teach. He is forever grateful to his professor for unlocking an untapped potential; he challenged William to question his true goal after completing the class. How far did William see himself going with this newfound exuberance to express himself? Or was he going to be another soul on ice, like the title of the Eldridge Cleaver eye-opening memoirs?

Pick up the Pace

Speak at a pace that is comfortable for both you and your audience. Avoid speaking too quickly or too slowly. We've all probably heard this short phrase said to us more than a few times in life: *"Pace yourself."* We should echo this to ourselves as much as possible when it comes to speaking opportunities. Realize that your best moments this season will be those that you live in and not the ones you rush through.

It's not far-fetched that any one person can become unnerved and easily fall into the mindset of *"I just want to get this over with."* It's understandable because this can be a symptom of low confidence in not only one's ability to present but also one's interest in their topic.

So, you find yourself on a stage-like setting, thinking to yourself, *'I need to hurry this along before they figure out I don't know what I'm doing up here.'* Confidence is the secret sauce we're going to continue to cover in this book.

One way to ensure you have your fair share of it is to practice memorizing your speech many times over. Record yourself and time yourself so you know, at the very least, you'll be prepared. Then, on the other side of the equation, an overconfident speaker can tend to drag the presentation out, misreading their audience's initial interest level and ending up losing their attention altogether. Normally you'll see people slowly getting up and walking out of the room, trying not to be noticed. We've all done it before, and if not, we've all wanted to.

Rushing is not the answer, and neither is tarrying on for too long. Both will cause you to miss the mark. Of course, *the Tortoise and the Hare* had two different philosophies approaching the race, and true enough, the tortoise did win. Slow and steady may have been his formula, but the word *'steady'* is the more important of the two. You just remember you're not in a race; you're in a dance. So, you should choose your words like you choose your steps within the rhythm and pick your spots to be swift and ease into your leisure.

Reginald Hill said, *"Pace doesn't mean speed. It means the right speed. Diagnosis and cure are simple. If you've reached where you want to be in your story too quickly, ask yourself what you've left out.*

If you've come to a certain point too slowly, ask yourself what kept you so long."

When people have conversations, there is a natural progression of information exchange. Be confident in what you bring to the table, and share your ideas like you're just talking with a friend.

Toni... Tony... Tone

Use your tone of voice to convey your emotions and to connect with your audience. If you've ever had the chance to attend an exercise class, you'll notice several things pretty quickly before you begin the session.

First, you'll notice who's taking the class with you, then what type of shape they're in compared to yourself. Not just that but you'll also tune into the instructor, their shape, as well as standing energy. After the session begins, one thing you certainly catch on to is the instructor's ability to have a commanding presence in the room. Whether the music is going or not, a great instructor will be able to convince you within the first few minutes if this class is for you while motivating you to give your all and want to come back for more the next day. Instant rapport was built, and it was made by the use of the instructor's tone. Whether you know it or not, they were able to help you feel a part of a community simply by the energy behind the sound of their voice. Their tone and not necessarily their words is the tool that creates the bond.

Co-author and speaker of this book, Cory Brazier, has first-hand experience with this concept because another passion of his is health and fitness. Besides the role he plays in *Gentlemen and Scholars* mentoring, he co-owns a business—*BrazierFit Boxing*—where he teaches classes to the community with his dad, Harold Brazier—a former World Class Professional Boxing Champion. Throughout the years, after conducting thousands of classes, Cory has found out that the success of the class had everything to do with his excitement, his commitment, and his motivation, which at the time was unknowingly communicated through his tone.

As a mindset mentor, he has always understood that the momentum he creates in the minds of others will help them carry themselves through the trials of doubt. His public speaking platform is one that reaches the everyday person struggling to maintain consistency in their physical fitness and all-around well-being journey. With that, he is tasked to show his students that on the other side of tribulation is jubilation. Cory realized that if he was going to benefit the improvement of his people's health, he was going to have to make sure his tone grips them enough to drag them along to reach their personal goals.

The tone is the control and the trust found in the energy of your voice. Make a habit of checking your energy, attitude, and mindset before you speak over others' lives so it can't be mistaken for anything else but positivity. As for us, we only want to speak life.

See Your Reflection

It Mirrors the Inflection:

A momentary mirror, in many ways, voice inflection, is one of those exciting subtleties that give the right amount of personality implanted mid-discussion that makes so much of a difference in just a few little seconds when it's unbridled. It's like the vocal version of the Joker's erratic energy peeking out of the bar windows, witnessing brief freedom, then laughing while being walked back to its cell. That stored-up vigor can be used as if it's a syringe on a fading patient, a perfectly timed shot of adrenaline injected for the ears to wake up their attention span.

Use inflection to emphasize certain words or phrases and convey the meaning of your message. The emphasis on a syllable and the cadences is just the delightful chaos that makes speech spin away from the mundane noise category. The balance of verbal peaks and valleys, zeniths and crescendos, like an opera of sorts, is where the main characters, through the medium of singing, raise and or lower the expectations of their audience.

The person who invites their audience to go on a journey must carry the voice of a leader. You can't afford to lose them, or they might lose their way. They're trusting you with their time, not so that you can entertain them but so you can help them grow. They count on you to help them make themselves to be more, have more and give more to this life. So, a calculated spike in your voice will assure them that you're passionate and serious about them being in your presence.

Pronunciation (Pronounce-to-a-Nation!)

We can all probably speak to the fact that it's easy to fall into a condition of mediocrity. When you're not focused or prepared, you tend to want to get the task over with, and most likely overlook things.

One thing that slips by us is the way we begin to talk when we're not engaged in the moment. We get sloppy with our wordplay without even recognizing it while forgetting how we're still in a performance of sorts. The bottom line is we want you to sound educated at all times. No matter what's going on in your mind, you need to have practiced your speech enough. If you're electing to use a word, then practice sounding it out enough to give it its due justice. Correct pronunciation of a word is where unseen powers reside in the details.

In some circles, it is believed that words are the gateway to magical outcomes. People who study mysticism understand that there lies an untapped energy within the essence of them. The potential for creating and manipulating follows behind soundwaves. It has even been suggested that embedded in the language are actual spells being casted, some more potent than others. We wouldn't say it's anything to be alarmed about, just something to be aware of because the average person is either clueless of this or just careless of it altogether.

Let's entertain this thought for a bit. Now, if we were actually casting spells with every word and syllable we uttered and were oblivious to it, think how much damage would be inflicted outward by speaking over someone's life in ignorance of this fact? Even worse, how much damage would we cause in our own lives? It's crazy because nowadays, people mispronounce even the nonsense they speak. But let's go back to the previous point about the magic that dwells in words. Hypothetically speaking, just like in those movies, when the sorcerer is distracted, he fumbles the words to a spell, and moments later, as a result, the undesired aftermath is realized and emerges.

The point of this section is to get you to understand that whether you believe it or not, each element of your words holds power. There needs to be an untainted focus when it comes to the pronunciation of each said term. If it is true, which we're not claiming it to be, that each word holds its ability to transform circumstances, then we should treasure them. Yet, just to be safe, we'll be treating them like they're flammable hazmat materials—try to handle them with care.

Make an effort to slow down and pronounce your words correctly, syllable by syllable, with clarity each time you have an opportunity to give a presentation. The meanings behind these sounds are not a plaything in the world of affirmations. To be candid, the techniques we're sharing aren't as important as the wisdom you must have when attaining them. Again, pronounce the words in a suitable manner because their power is in the details.

Needless to say, but we'll still say it: by practicing these voice techniques, you can improve your public speaking skills and effectively convey your distinctive message to your audience.

Remember: Give your audience the same energy that you want to receive.

Think of it as a conversation between you and the audience. If you can carry on a fluid conversation with two or more people, you can certainly give a great speech. Whether your audience consists of two people or two thousand, whether you're talking about the latest life achievement or what you did today at work, be yourself, talk directly to people, and make a connection memorable with them.

In fact, if you're in the educational field, such as a teacher, principal, and have a heart for your students, then you might want to consider this*: The Scholars Speak Program,* which we offer as an option for kids in every school district, is a direct line into the agency in which the youth are able to share their voice on various topics and have opportunities to get paid for it.

If you know a child with potential, reach out to us at gentlemenandscholarsinc.com or our other social media platforms and introduce them to this information. You might be the liaison they never knew they needed... *Scholar UP!*

"Only the prepared speaker deserves to be confident."

~ **Dale Carnegie**

Chapter Seven:
Going Through the Fire BREEDS…

CONFIDENCE

Will's Story - The Spelling Bee

In 1986, while in his eighth-grade classroom, young William Douglas, founder of *Gentlemen and Scholars Inc.,* was about to have his life altered. Sitting at his desk, attentive to his studies, he noticed his teacher approaching him with an optimistic look on her face. Somewhat perplexed, he kept his head down and acted as if he wasn't aware that she stopped and stood over him.

"Congratulations, William," she spoke. *"You've been nominated to participate in a school-wide Spelling Bee."*

After hearing this from her, William pretended as if he didn't hear it—all while a conversation was being had on the inside of him. *"Is she serious? Nah, can't be, she said my name, maybe she'll move on to someone else, but she's still standing here... Why me, ugh? Maybe if I don't respond, she'll walk away."*

"William, did you hear me?" She reiterated. *"You've been nominated to be in our school Spelling Bee."*

"Yes, ma'am," William said. *"I heard you, but I'm going to have to respectfully decline. I don't wanna do it."*

"But William, I wish that you would reconsider this great opportunity." His teacher elaborated.

But William's mind was made up, and he thought no more of it because he knew that while honorable enough to be challenged to be in a Spelling Bee, his peer group would think differently. Most likely, he'd be bullied and made fun of. So basically, the fear of being ostracized by his peers prevented him from accepting the invitation.

Ironically, William had a hands-on mother who, in addition to his homework, implored him to study words from the dictionary throughout his grade school years. What William didn't know was that between the time of leaving school and arriving home, his teacher had called his mother and told her about the Spelling Bee. This very act here is to be noted and we'll come back to it later on in the book.

So, finally arriving home, while walking in the door from school, William's mother emphatically stated to him, *"You're in that Spelling Bee!"* Blindsided, William was stunned but received his mother's charge as she encouraged him to take advantage of any and every opportunity to *"let his light shine."*

She understood the importance of words, communication, and expressing oneself. She knew that wherever there was a stage, there was a chance to share an idea while building confidence in oneself. A Spelling Bee is no different than a school assembly that showcases the most interesting information. William complied with his mother's request, and out of one hundred and fifty students, William came in first runner-up.

Now, this accomplishment did a few things for William. It proved to him that he was smart and could compete academically as well as athletically. The experience forever changed the trajectory of his life.

The opportunity to speak publicly amongst peers, school faculty, and parents gave William great confidence and the ability to express himself.

We all know that feeling or believing that one can rely on someone or something, see that is called a *firm trust*. The feeling of self-assurance arising from one's appreciation of one's ability or qualities, now that is confidence. It's essential to have confidence, but it's not easily attained. Confidence is what sets apart an unsure talker from a masterful speaker. It is the secret sauce. You can be knowledgeable and an expert in any subject, but if you don't believe that you are a worthy deliverer, then the message itself will be lost in the sound.

Just like William, we all must participate in our own rescue. Confidence is built by repetitive actions and the logging of time while involved in the proper activity. Saying yes to as many opportunities as possible to speak, even if it's just in front of your family and friends, will incrementally increase one's ability to speak more confidently.

Chapter Eight:
Innate To Engage

"The success of your presentation will be judged, not by the knowledge you send, but by what the listener receives."

~ **Lilly Walters**

Public speaking can be one of the most challenging yet rewarding forms of communication. To be successful, you need to know how to engage your audience.

Here are a few tips for doing just that:

Start Strong

You should always open with a statement that introduces your subject in such a way that it intrigues them. The opener should have a spark that ignites people to want to learn more, which causes them to lean forward, and then you begin to develop your subject. Be very clear and get them interested. It's not about you; it's all about *them.*

We've stirred up many audiences with the use of our calling card, "Scholar Up." Before we even get started with the presentation, we make sure everyone in the house knows we're going to proceed on one accord. All eyes watch as we enter the stage and pause for a moment of silence. Then comes our 10-second attention indicator: we say, "This is serious, everyone, quickly now..." index finger pointed skyward and with a united voice, "everyone, all together... Scholar Up!!!" The energy never leaves, but just in case it does, we inject another few doses halfway through our talks.

The first few minutes of your presentation are critical in making a good first impression. Start with an interesting story, a thought-provoking question, a humorous statement, or a light joke. All of these are potent options and actually may be what sets you apart from any speech they've heard prior to them giving you their ear. Leading with icebreakers will grab the attention of your audience and increase their engagement with your message. Activating feelings as early as possible will make you memorable at the beginning.

Even Maya Angelou said, *"People will forget what you said, forget what you did, but won't forget how you made them feel."*

The Picturesque ~~~~ Use Visuals

Whoever said, *"A picture is worth a thousand words,"* had a definite foresight into public speaking because we found that this is the case in so many instances. So, we like to say make sure you give the substance and the show.

With that said, there are three common styles of learning that people pattern themselves after, which include auditory, kinesthetic, and visual. First, let's cover the auditory stimulated mind, which means a person's hearing of the information helps them process it the best. The second is the kinesthetic. This pathway is the dominant learning of feeling and using the hands-on experience to be the most beneficial for them. Third is the visual. This pathway allows the mind to be most comfortable in retaining outer messages through what the eyes see. They are all playing a very important role in the functions of a person's comprehension dynamic. We've discovered that not one is more potent than the other, but one stands out as most requested when giving a presentation—the visual approach.

When public speaking, specifically, the background images connect an observer to what they're listening to. The visual helps drive home a point more when coupled with the voice (auditory) of a speaker. Some, if not most, people learn better through visual aids. For this reason, people can actually see themselves as living and experiencing the drama within your presentation. Their faculty of sight preps them to relate to your proposal of ideas. It's an understatement of how important it is to consider setting up complimentary illustrations because the imagery mixed with the voice allows for achieving maximum attention.

Visuals are an effective way to illustrate your point while keeping your audience engaged.

- Graphs

- Diagrams

- Flow Charts

- Hand Outs

- Maps

- Video Clips

- Guides

- Pictures

- PowerPoint/Slide Show Presentation

Pull out all the stops, and don't allow anyone to leave your presence feeling unsatisfied. Visuals can help break up the monotony of a long presentation and make your message more memorable. Yes, the picture is worth a thousand words, and seeing is believing.

Gain Traction by Allowing for Interaction

We'll probably reinforce concepts over and over again throughout this motivational guide. One that we recommend, which, if applied often, will never fail, is approaching speeches like conversations. Not just one side, though. Think of it like getting to know a blind date on the other side of a wall. The only way to see them is to request from them the energy you need to drive the conversation. Force your listeners to walk outside of their comfort zone. Don't wait for them to give you permission; just pull them into your universe. Usually, people think they're going to be served a platter of information, but what they don't know is that by stepping into the chef's kitchen, sharing the very ingredient that they use to keep themselves engaged is like putting their love in the meal and might give it the flavor it needs. (Now That's Food For The Soul)

Ask your audience questions or lure them to participate in a discussion, which will help them stay present and will make your presentation more dynamic. Have you ever heard a preacher use the *"turn to your neighbor and say…"* right in the middle of their sermon? Or a *"repeat after me"* phrase? Or even a *"raise your hand if this happens to you"* type of volunteering motion? All of this inherent interaction is what innates the engagement of your audience to take ownership of the speech you're delivering.

Chapter Nine:
Body Has Dialect

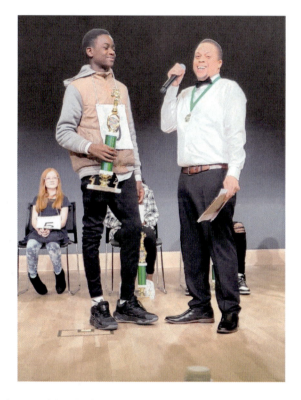

Your voice and body language can be powerful tools for engaging your audience. Speak with confidence, maintain eye contact, and use gestures that help emphasize your points.

Body language is a crucial aspect of public speaking because it enhances the effectiveness of your speech and helps you give a more powerful presentation. The more in tune you are with the body's parlance gives the appearance of confidence and authority—indicating that you're in control. With proper mannerisms it helps to establish your credibility and makes the audience more likely to trust and believe in the message being presented.

Effective body language demonstrates professionalism and preparedness. It shows that you put the time and thought into your presentation, enhancing your overall visual image. The visual impact of gestures, movements, and expressions helps the audience stay attentive and retain the information presented. You can use body language to help emphasize your points and make your message clearer. Gestures, facial expressions, and movements add a visual element that complements the verbal part of your speech.

Our intention talks through our energy and our energy talks through our vessel. The body carries the cargo of the offering soul that reaches the soul in need. Engaging body language is what makes a presentation more memorable. The dialect of the body shows emotions more effectively than words alone; it adds another dimension to your presentation. Facial expressions and gestures can express enthusiasm, passion, concern, and other emotions, making the message more relatable and interesting.

We talk about managing nerves in this book. Body language can also help manage nervousness. Focusing on maintaining good posture, using intentional gestures, and making eye contact can help turn nervous energy into positive and effective communication. It's not a convoluted process at all. Don't get too carried away with body language; we don't want you constantly moving, waving, twisting, and jumping during your presentation because too much can be a distraction to your overall message.

Here are some examples of a few key body language movements and gestures that are important in public speaking:

The Upward Gesture

This gesture can help lift the energy of the audience. Gestures directed upwards can signify excitement, inspiration, and motivation. It can also assist in a call to action. Have you ever been to a ball game or watched one on TV? You might have noticed someone from the team using upward gestures with their arms and hands to ignite energy to get cheers from the crowd.

Forward Face

Face your audience directly when making important points. Turning your body towards the audience shows a sense of rapport, engagement, and confidence. Never turn your back to the audience; not only will you lose the momentum of your presentation by losing eye contact, but it makes it harder for your audience to focus on your presentation. If you don't have a microphone, it may be troublesome for your audience to hear you if your back is turned.

These are just a couple of examples. By using body gestures, it gives a better stage presence and you can take your public speaking experience to the next level and have a more positive impact on your audience.

The Greater Good of Nervousness Excitement

Public speaking is one of the most common fears among people—next to the fear of death or running into a burning building. Even though you may feel nervous—those unwanted butterflies that flutter in your stomach—it is possible to manage that fear and become a confident and effective speaker. Public speaking can be very intimidating for many people, but it doesn't have to be. It can all work for the greater good of your development process. In fact, with the right preparation and mindset, you can make public speaking a relatively stress-free experience.

Co-author S. R. Williams I was known for his intelligence, creativity, free-spirited, easy-going personality, and kind heart. However, despite his many talents, Shane had one great fear that overshadowed everything else: public speaking. Shane's fear stemmed when he was a kid from an incident in his local church, where his dad, Reverend Sylvester Williams Jr., is the pastor. Shane had to present an Easter speech in front of the whole congregation.

He was extremely nervous and trembling; he stumbled over his words, his face turned red, and his voice was barely a whisper. The other kids and some adults snickered, and the memory of their laughter haunted him for years. As time passed, Shane avoided any situation that required him to speak in public. He turned down opportunities, avoided social gatherings, and even refrained from sharing his thoughts in class at school or any speaking opportunities at church. The fear of repeating that embarrassing moment held him back from pursuing many of his dreams.

Since his dad was the Pastor, Shane couldn't run from it for long; it was time for those Easter speeches again. The thought of reciting his speech aloud in front of an audience once again filled him with dreadful anxiety. He tried everything he could to get out of the assignment but his parents weren't letting up. But something inside him had changed—Shane was tired of being held back by his fear. He realized that if he wanted to grow as a person and chase his dreams, he needed to confront his fear head-on.

He spent weeks preparing—studying his material, visualizing, practicing in front of a mirror, and recording his voice to improve his delivery. His mother helped him by being his audience and providing constructive feedback, which boosted his confidence. The day of the speech arrived, and Shane's heart pounded profusely with anxiety— his hands clammy, his throat dry, and his stomach started to twist and turn to the point of discomfort.

But, as he saw the microphone and the familiar setup, he took a deep breath and looked around the room, meeting the encouraging eyes of members of the audience. He remembered why he was there:

to present his speech and connect with others. He remembered all the hard work he had put in. He reminded himself of the progress he had made and wanted to show his audience how much he improved.

When it was his turn, Shane stepped up to the microphone. His voice was shaky at first, but as he continued, he found his rhythm. He spoke clearly and with confidence, and his passion for speaking and storytelling came shining through. The audience was impressed by his authenticity and natural ability to express himself in front of an audience.

Let Shane's story be an inspiration to many. He learned that the first step in overcoming any fear is often the hardest, but it is also the most crucial. By facing his fear of public speaking, Shane opened up a world of possibilities for himself, proving that courage, preparation, and perseverance can lead to personal growth and fulfillment.

Although there are many ways to overcome and manage nervousness, here are just a few tips for the greater good of you speaking on the public scene.

1. Prep-Formation

Preparation is key when it comes to public speaking. Make sure you know your material well and have practiced your presentation multiple times to reduce the chances of you forgetting something. Your level of readiness will help you to be more confident in your presentation which can help reduce anxiety and nerves to make your delivery more natural and engaging. Preparation helps reduce the fear of the unknown; a lot of times, we're nervous because we don't know what to expect. When you know your material and have practiced thoroughly, you feel more in control. The more familiar you are with your topic, the more confident you'll feel when it comes time to speak.

Preparation ensures a clear structure. A well-prepared speech has an intro, middle, and close, with each section flowing seamlessly into the next. This clarity helps the audience follow along with you and understand your message. A well-prepared speech reflects your commitment and respect for your audience. It shows that you value their time and are serious about your message.

~Random Punch in The Arm Tip by Brian Tracy

A DEDICATION TO PREPARATION

Preparation is the beginning, middle, and end.

Preparation is 90% of your success in speaking. It means that you think on paper. You write it down and organize your words. Practice. Practice. Practice. Be serious. Then, you'll be at liberty to speak freely. Keep it simple.

a. Tell them what you're going to tell them.

b. Tell them.

c. Then, tell them what you told them.

Now, carry on.

The Gentlemen and Scholars Inc. initiatives have far surpassed any obstacles placed as deterrence with the proven track record of readying our steps. In conclusion, preparation is the foundation of a successful speech. It enables you to deliver your message clearly and confidently, engage your audience effectively, and handle any challenges that arise. By investing time in thorough preparation, you set yourself up for success and leave a lasting, positive impression on your audience.

"More preparation eliminates poor presentation. #Bar"

2. I Must Foresee What Is for Me

By the way of your mind's eye, foreseeing yourself giving a successful presentation can also help reduce your nervousness. Picture yourself being applauded after delivering a great discourse, and focus on the aspect of feeling a positive emotional reinforcement from the experience.

A healthy habit of practicing, whether you're preparing to speak or not, is positive self-talk—affirmations. Before you give your speech, take a few moments to focus on positive affirmations. Do it so far ahead of a speaking engagement that by the time the event comes around, they'll already be anchored within you. Remind yourself of your strengths and why you are the right person to give this speech. Visualization helps you hone in on the task at hand. By mentally rehearsing your speech, you can reinforce your focus on delivering your message effectively rather than being distracted by potential fears or doubts.

Exercising the foresight component of your imagination is the cornerstone of mental scrimmage. Just as athletes use visualization to practice their skills, speakers can use it to rehearse their speeches. This mental practice can improve your delivery, timing, and overall performance. Visualizing success helps you cultivate a positive mindset. This positive outlook can translate into greater enthusiasm and energy during your actual speech, making you more engaging and persuasive. *(Remember: the energy you give your audience is the same energy they'll give you in return.)* Feeding off their reciprocation will help to boost your self-confidence and take your mind off your edginess.

In a nutshell, inwardly picturing success is a valuable tool for public speaking. It can boost your confidence, reduce tension, improve focus, and help you mentally rehearse your speech. By fostering a positive mindset and preparing yourself for success, visualization can enhance your overall performance, help you get that Monumental Mouthpiece, and make your public speaking experience more rewarding and enjoyable.1

3. Zeroing In on Your Attendees

Focusing on the ones who have assembled before you is crucial for effective public speaking. It helps in several ways, making your speech more engaging and relevant and giving a lasting impression on your audience.

Understand your audience's interests, needs, and expectations. When you prioritize your audience's needs, your speech is more likely to provide them with valuable insights, information, motivation, and inspiration. Whom you deem important increases the likelihood that your message will have a lasting impact on them. Tailoring your speech to your audience makes it more relevant and engaging, ensuring that your message resonates with your audience.

When you consider your audience, you are more likely to use techniques that maintain their interest, such as storytelling, humor, and interactive elements. Engaged audiences are more likely to retain information and respond positively to your message. Giving full attention to your audience allows you to anticipate potential challenges or questions from the audience and plan your responses. This readiness helps you handle unexpected situations that cause heightened nervousness.

Instead of emphasizing on your apprehension, shift your focus to the gravity of the moment. Think more on how you can connect with your audience and make your presentation interesting. Redirect your focal point to the cementing of your presence in their memory. This maneuver can be done simply by inviting them in to become a transient authority over the energy of your commentary. After all, they are there to listen to you, so focus on engaging them. Subtle interactions with your crowd will help you to forget your uneasiness and focus on delivering a great presentation.

In conclusion, making your audience the focal point is a fundamental aspect of successful public speaking. It enhances relevance, builds connection, increases engagement, and boosts your confidence, which helps you to overcome nervousness. By understanding and addressing your audience's needs, you can deliver a speech that is not only impressive but also memorable.

4. The Lasting Gasp

Whenever you're perturbed and the angst starts to take hold, take a few deep breaths to help yourself relax. This book contains some things that deserve a second look. Some subjects need a double portion so you can see just how high a priority we consider them to be. The meditative foundation of breathing is what draws in a wandering mind to be still. Let it sink in.

The breath must be mastered, not just for speech but for life. The depths of the mindful intake of air before you declare your truth speak volumes of how your posture will be throughout your presentation. Taking yawning type breaths, in particular, is a simple yet effective technique that can significantly help you with twitchiness for your public speaking assignment. It's the impetus or the force in the shadows that helps reduce stress, anxiety, and those unwanted butterflies—in other words, your nerves! This calming effect can make you feel more relaxed and less jittery before and during your speech.

Slowly yet calmly intaking a vast amount of air can help clear your mind, allowing you to focus better on your speech and your audience. This increased focus helps you to stay positive to get the best out of the moment and stay present and engaged with your audience. Deep breaths increase the oxygen flow to your brain and body, which can help you feel more alert. It helps you bring your best energy to have a deeper connection with your audience. To connect is to touch, and touch is how we feel.

Try it now! Take a deep breath. Now, blow it out at a calm, steady pace. Try inhaling for six seconds, holding that air for four seconds, then exhaling for six seconds, repeating as often as necessary. Practice deep breathing regularly with intention. Not only will it help you in public speaking, but it will help you relax in every aspect of your life!

In conclusion, deep breaths are a valuable tactic for public speaking. It lessens tension, enhances focus, improves voice control, and increases oxygen flow. By adding deep breathing into your preparation and delivery, you can significantly improve your public speaking performance and feel more confident and relaxed. #yougotthis

Chapter Ten:
Take Form & Scholar UP

(IT SPEAKS FOR ITSELF)

According to the Oxford Languages definition, a 'scholar' is *a specialist in a particular branch of study, especially the humanities; a distinguished academic.* It is a term usually used to describe a person who is highly educated or has an aptitude for studying. We've found that the word is often used in this context as a way to describe the likes of any intellectual, but notwithstanding, it can also be used to highlight an expert in any career field. So, it's from this standpoint we're going to speak to how being a scholar is universal per se.

One way to look at it is that it's probably the very thing in your life that is most interesting to you—professional or recreational—that you can explain to anyone the ins and outs of without putting much thought into it. In a sense, you can be considered somewhat of an expert in that field and, at the very least, qualified to speak on it.

To be a specialist in any area of life is applaudable, if only because of the time you invested learning and knowing that subject enough to teach another. Once knowledge is acquired, it becomes an inner treasure with intrinsic value that not even the craftiest thief will prevail in robbing it from you. Making the responsibility of moving the wisdom along solely yours to pass down voluntarily for the sake of progression, and to be added upon. So, to be a specialist is to be an expert, which is to be a scholar, and we encourage all to seek ways to accomplish this title. A scholar is one who masters. It makes no difference the background of a person.

We can hear you now saying what's in it for me? It's the question you might ask as pushback to becoming well-versed in something that already interests you. You'd be right to ask this because let's face it, incentive is the driving force behind any motivation. What are you going to get out of it? There are so many benefits to achieving a mastery level in your craft, but we'll list a few shallow ones. By evolving into a scholar in any scope of life, chances you'll accumulate money, power, respect, notoriety, influence, fame, love, success, health, and healthy relationships increase exponentially. Howbeit, the benefits with more depth to them are more subtle and introduced throughout the book as hinges to enrichment that provides a satisfying personal esteem.

Sidenote:

If you're a professor at any college or university, this is a call to action pointed in your direction. You've earned your title because you've understood, performed, and achieved high ranks in public speaking usage. The students you lecture will need to be thoroughly adept at public debating and impromptu speeches, along with a sleuth of other soft skills needed for their future. This book would definitely add to the dynamic of your course curriculum. Scholars Speak, our speaker's bureau's agency and program, might also be a helpful option to position them for extra credit or, at minimum, include this guide in your requirements of reading material.

We want to help people realize it doesn't matter what your passion in life is. Just become a scholar in it, and if you're not, then by all means, *Scholar Up!* If there's any information that holds your interest enough to devote any of your valuable time to, then it falls in the category of things that must be maximized. Why not become a scholar in that area? It may be the tool that creates a path that leads to your idea of freedom. Study what grabs your attention most, analyze it, make it your own; and if it's taking root within you, then it's only a matter of time before it's ready to bear fruit. Challenge yourself to dive deep and grow an unshakable self-assurance.

It really doesn't matter what subject you decide to Scholar Up in; just remember, from the abundance of the heart, the mouth speaks. Your age is a nonfactor. Your ability to Scholar Up will work for you as an asset, and this investment will prove its worth and return to you in more ways than typical wealth. The key is when you take ownership of it, like any other emotionally charged phrase, Scholar Up becomes a polarizing self-fulfilling prophecy. Thus, it's the very reason it serves as our calling card and affirmation of credence that can be universally utilized by those who wield it. It's likened to the legend of the mythical sword called Excalibur. Those of you who are familiar with the story of King Authur know that it took the one who was most worthy to lift the magical weapon out of the stone.

Scholar Up is the very battle cry, empowering the speaker who looks to pull confidence and reassurance out of their inner being, allowing them to establish a leader's identity and become the foremost version of their expressive self. Their sword is actually their voice, which is their victory, and this victory is yours to possess as well. As precious as it (their voice) is, it also seems to have been wedged long enough to become cryptic. Yet, the ability to pull it out of the hardened, unforgiving depths of doubt has absolutely nothing to do with one's strength. Now, let that sink in.

Yet, only the strength of one's mindset and heart matters. Once one's state of mind becomes in sync with one's passion, it gives energy to one's personal battle cry, which creates great power in wordplay.

List of Today's Best Public Speakers' Motivational Speakers

In this section, we want to point you in the direction of a few of our favorite notable public speakers. These presenters are at the very top of the motivational speaking industry. We encourage you to look them up, watch their videos, and do your research on their paths to success. They all have inspiring stories and great examples of reaching your full potential.

These are the models of the speaking sector and will be sure to have resources you can tap into so you can hone in on the polishing up of your skills. At the very least, you'll never run out of motivational material to inspire you. These are heavy hitters, so learn from them as much as you can. Too many to name so we chose those who are standing like monuments.

All of them are powerful in their own right, but like we said, these are only a few honorable mentions:

Tony Robbins	*Les Brown*
Simon Sinek	*Eric Thomas*
Dave Ramsey	*Louise Hay*
Seth Godin	*John Maxwell*
Nick Vujicic	*Dr. Tasha Eurich*
Ekhart Tollie	*Debra Searle*
Robert Kiyosaki	*Karl Lillrud*
Mel Robbins	*Sadhguru*
Brian Tracy	*Suze Orman*
Lisa Nichols	*Eddie Turner*
Grant Cardone	*Gary Vaynerchuk*
Darren Hardy	*Shiv Khera*
Deepak Chopra	*Peter Sage*
Chris Gardner	*Erica Dhawan*
Jack Canfield	*Jim Lawless*
David Goggins	*Boris Cherniak*
Duncan Stevens	*Chad Foster*
Iyanla Vanzant	*Steve Sims*
Amy Purdy	*Jill Sinclair*
Tim Grover	*Kevin Brown*
Jordan Belfort	*Jody Carrington*

Ryan Campbell   *Lynne Twist*

John O'Leary   *Marie Forleo*

Laura Gassner Otting   *Trent Shelton*

Brene Brown   *Vishen Lakhiani*

Ed Mylett   *Daymond John*

Jane Goodall   *Rich Roll*

Jay Shetty   *Andrew Huberman*

Tim Ferriss   *Paul Polman*

Sadie Robertson Huff   *Van Jones*

Lewis Howes   *Halima Aden*

Guy Kawasaki   *Janet Mock*

Glennon Doyle   *Brian Clement*

The Late Greats Spoke Life...

Jim Rohn   *Stephen Convey*

Wayne Dyer   *Reverend Ike*

Zig Ziglar   *Naomi Judd*

Chapter Eleven:
MONUMENTAL SPEECHES

Monuments hold historical importance because of their lasting effect on the ones fortunate enough to experience them. What stands as monumental is an imposing symbol of an ever-present impact. Mount Rushmore is a tribute to the idea of freedom, but it was designed to highlight and immortalize a group of leaders who established a nation's ways. There is significance in moving an agenda along with a team because the scaling efforts will almost ensure all bases will be covered. The benefits of being coordinated remain true in principles of speech building.

The broader the team you have access to, the broader the options of skill that's available. As long as everyone knows and plays their role, the puzzle will come together. Principles of speech writing and selection follow this rule of thumb as well, and it's easy to make a sport out of it.

A basketball realist is sure to appreciate and even agree with spicy sports takes, like when former NBA player Jalen Rose debated that *"The positions were only created so a novice could follow the game."*

There are different factors that make certain speakers more effective than others. One of those factors is the type of speech the speaker chooses to deliver. It all depends on their desired result, but they have multiple options for the most memorable showing. All forms of speeches play a key role in this, so we embrace them, carry them with us, and plug them in where they'll best fit to charge up the masses.

The Informative Speech

"Effective communication is 20% what you know and 80% how you feel about what you know."

~ Jim Rohn

Let us say first that it's important to understand that it's the person who makes the speech alive in its category. Every speech can contain a little bit of one category and a little bit of another, so it's unfair to define them by levels of impact. So not to our surprise, we've found that many people hold an internal excitement about acquiring information. Most people love to learn new things, so don't ever judge or look down on the power of one who informs.

An informative speech, by definition, is an educational approach through the use of facts and evidence so you can establish proper credibility for your topic. According to an article from the SAGE Flex for Public Speaking, *"...an effective informative speech informs the audience about a specific topic in one of four interesting and memorable ways."* These four approaches include definitions, explanations, descriptions, and demonstrations, and for added interest, they can also include visual images.

But who said meticulousness can't be fascinating? If not, at the very least, it could be labeled indispensable. The speaker who aims to enlighten by sharing facts and figures can sway a heavy crowd in any direction they choose because their advantage is in their abstract expertise. They should focus on unique objects, events, processes, concepts, and examples. Some of the most skilled presenters tell a great story with only data-driven subjects supported by graphs, charts, and PowerPoint visuals. They are able to tell this story through the language of numbers (which is said to never lie), accompanied by statistics, always finding a way to paint the pictures to the groups of people with the tendency to trust without proof.

You'll usually know when the result you seek with an audience has been met by the end of your speech. If you go with the intent to teach, more than likely, the listeners will be open to learning. Informative speeches are usually found in classrooms by teachers, lecture halls by professors, seminar settings by professionals, and even in employment spaces by human resource administrations. The point is that anyone can present a speech that informs the public about issues that need to be addressed now or in the future. Everyone is qualified to speak in this format; you only need to prepare your materials, your information, and yourself.

The Inspiring Speech

"The highest human act is to inspire."

While being interviewed as a special guest on the Rap Radar Podcast, the iconic late rapper, artist, and businessman Nipsey Hussle uttered these words. He went on to say what factor really played a major part in his liking music. He elaborated that music offered so many different kinds of beneficial messages, but for him, it was the music that inspired him. He explained that *"...it inspires you to dance, it inspires you to get some money, it inspires you to fall in love, but it inspires you."*

The inspiring speech is delivered with the purpose of stimulating confidence in the pursuit of worthy goals while instilling an optimistic perspective to succeed in them. Inspiration comes from internal sources, which is what the speaker targets for the sake of stirring them up. When the stage invites its guests, their words settle into the minds of their audience with the intention of creating an elevated emotional experience.

The inspirational speech is called upon with the aim to drive us to *"the meaningful something"* and to take satisfying action towards it. Its persuasion is structured just enough to be uplifting while promoting changed behavior. This type of speech is not as easy as it seems because the desired results are unpredictable. Some of the most influential and inspiring speeches in American history were given with the intent to grab the soul. Described in many cases as the ones that should be studied, these *"aha"* moments of outpouring left us positively shaken as a people. The *Gettysburg Address* (1863) by *Abraham Lincoln, Martin Luther King Jr.'s I Have A Dream* 1963, *Steve Jobs How To Live Before You Die* (2005), and *Barack Obama's Yes We Can* (2008) are just a few that we can all learn from because their outcomes had a modern-day viral effect.

One never knows who is in attendance and for what reason they are there. It's difficult to forecast who will leave inspired because everyone is not looking to be. But for the ones who are, all you have to remember is to bring your credibility and your passion because what comes from the heart reaches the heart. Now, it's important to mention that even without passion, the inspirational approach can be effective. Just like with anything, you can fake this passion and still get a rise out of the crowd.

But why not step out in front of the people who need it most with the intent to give an anecdote and with the intent to give of yourself? We want you to exit from the stage, leaving people whispering about you, saying, *"Wow, he was deep in his bag like the fries were at the bottom."* You will be paid in ways money can't grant you. No one really knows how many people they inspire when they grace the microphone. Jim Rohn used to thank his onlookers no matter how many there were. He knew that the one that is inspired takes you with them ironically as they leave with you.

In an experience of virtuous connection, you are all a part of each other's success stories now. Strangely, somehow, they'll never let you forget them. The reason is they now have a strong urge to want to make you proud of them, they'll find a way to make a mark in this world that attributes to what you planted in them. So, the highest human act will be achieved.

The Transformational Speech

The transformative speech is the perennial all-star of all speeches because people actually proposition within themselves after hearing you speak to their core values. The world of public speaking is vast in its ability to provoke true change. We may be biased, but we believe in it more than any other form of soft skills offered. The monumental mouthpiece is on full display when these kinds of speeches are delivered to the masses.

To help transform someone into their enhanced future self is to first know that a better version is possible for them to become. You must also be able to convince them to accept that this better version potentially exists now. You, as a speaker, should know there is no tool you don't have access to. Recognizing that incorporating what is informative, inspiring and motivational can all contribute to the transformation your audience is seeking for their lives. The residual effect of seeking reform is what overpowers the problems; the solution lingers in the minds, and the action steps follow like a shadow, reminding them of your words.

When you build upon the stories of your past experiences and share your journey of why and how you made a shift, it drives home the promises they made to themselves to change. It's what's called a *lasting* speech—it endures through the tough trials and the seasons of self-doubt, recurring the inner themes that survive the outer voices.

The transformative speech acts as an extended affirmation anchored in the minds and hearts of people, cementing a commitment to going in a new direction. When the hype of the event is over, and the emotions have died down, the message continues to touch that person. If they really heard you, they'll go home and be convicted within themselves.

The transformative speech does have a secret sauce containing 7 ingredients. Yes, your **Opener** is important, your **Introduction** is key, your **Credibility** is critical, your **Optimism** pivotal, your **Achievable Objectives** are essential, your **Confirmation** over them is imperative, giving them **Alternatives** is necessary, and your **Conclusion** is major. With all that said, be the change you're looking to see in the world (it's speech-worthy) and then convince them they can do the same, and they'll transform in due season.

The Motivational Speech

"Speak now or forever, hold your peace" is a requisition that gives the witnesses a chance to speak out and oppose the uniting of the two. Laying claim of your hold or release of power. The motivational speech gives its listeners a glimpse of two futures. Both wield a high price. It's hard to pay the price of neglect because you've just purchased a lifetime of regret along with the *"if only I would have..."* receipt, the inner voice that reminds you what could have been.

Now, the cost of just taking action and doing it can be expensive, as well. The sacrifices of hard work are the price to pay for the opportunity to experience your brightest moment. It'll be hard to write the speech, dedicate the hours to practice it, and muster up the courage to face the possibility of embarrassment or a standing ovation.

YOU ARE A MOTIVATIONAL SPEAKER.

The techniques we share in this book are only to help you realize this fact about yourself. Being motivational in your wordplay happens automatically when you permit yourself to be great. You are here for your people and to give your people the motive to succeed.

The public speaking mogul and author Eric ET Thomas is considered the world's number one motivational speaker. After listening to him work his magic, one thing is constant: he is here to win in life, whether you choose to or not, so why aren't you choosing to? He motivates by using his pulling force of common sense matched with his intense coaching energy. He's reminding people all over the world that no one can stop what you allow to be released from inside. Speak now or forever, hold your peace. Remember, the crowd could give you nothing, and you must give them everything. The energy is what rules the room.

The motivational speech has its components: an engaging opening, an authentic personal story of elevation, compelling quotes, the emotional element, meaningful humor, content with depth, inspiring conclusions, and a call to action. The energy is what rules the room above all.

Retired psychologist, author, and platform speaker Dr. Mardy Grothe said, "Words have incredible power. They can make people's hearts soar, or they can make people's hearts sore."

We've all been moved by someone's words before; what we didn't realize is that we have that same moving ability if we choose to step into it. We're in the age of the motivational speaker. Everyone from the YouTuber to the life coach, actor, celebrity, reformed felon, distinguished educator, to the rags-to-riches accomplished business professional, etc., can see themselves on the big stage receiving applause. We love it. We implore you to first be the motivational action the world hasn't seen yet and then Speak on it!

The Impromptu Speech

Once you've exercised and practiced these tips in this book, you'll be able to have fun with the impromptu speech. The impromptu speech is one delivered without prior preparation or planning. Sometimes, the speaker may be put on the spot with a related or unrelated topic or unexpected event that you didn't plan for. It requires you to quickly adjust and organize your thoughts and present them clearly in the moment.

Impromptu speeches are given with little to no advance notice to the speaker. The speaker must rely on their ability to think quickly and clearly under pressure to deliver a good presentation. The speaker must be able to adapt to the context and audience, tailoring their speech to fit the situation and the listeners' interests and expectations. These speeches are usually short, often lasting just a few minutes. Impromptu speaking is often used in various settings, such as the classroom, meetings, interviews, debates, and social gatherings.

There's an old scripture that says: *'Be ready in season and out of season..'* meaning be prepared at all times, even when it's unexpected or inconvenient.

Here are a few tips to help you tackle and be ready for your next impromptu speech:

If you're responding to a question or a previous speaker, *listen carefully* to ensure you understand the topic or context. Before you start your speech, *ask questions* to help you understand the topic and the context. Questions also give you extra time to get your thoughts together for the unexpected moment.

Draw from your own experiences. The information that you've studied and prepared in the past is stored up in you. Draw from that well of knowledge that you've learned along the way to help you in this moment of spontaneity. The creativity that lives in the unscripted can lead your impulse to find relevant and relatable content to include in your speech.

Have you ever heard of the famous saying, *"Stay ready so you don't have to get ready?"* Staying ready is a great way to combat procrastination. By staying ready, you stay alert, and it gives you a sense of urgency to not wait until the last minute to prepare because you're already prepared to at least touch on a topic. You may not know enough to go into great detail on the subject, but you know enough to get you through this impromptu moment.

Remember, during an impromptu speech, try to stick to the *main points* and avoid rambling. If you start rambling, you'll find yourself going down a rabbit hole that you might not be able to come back from. Being concise gives you the most impact and helps keep your speech focused.

Practice Regularly. The more you practice impromptu speaking, the more you will improve your ability to think quickly on your feet and articulate your words and thoughts clearly during your speech.

Engage in activities that force you to practice impromptu, like joining random conversations, participating in debates, or practicing with friends. Even without proper preparation, try to organize your speech into a clear structure:

- **Intro:** Start with a brief introduction of the topic.

- **Body:** Present two to three main points.

- **Close:** Summarize your points and end with a strong closing statement or ask, "Are there any more questions?"

Lastly, stay calm. Take a deep breath to calm your nerves before you begin speaking. Maintaining composure helps you think more clearly and gives a presence of control.

In conclusion, impromptu speaking is a valuable skill that can enhance your ability to communicate effectively in unexpected situations. By listening, asking questions, drawing from your own experiences, staying calm, and practicing regularly, you'll be able to organize your thoughts and become skilled at delivering great impromptu speeches. Thus giving you a *"Monumental Mouthpiece."*

The Informative. The Inspiring. The Transformative. The Motivational. The Impromptu. All possess Mount Rushmore's towering effect by lifting its presenters to a higher ground. We chose to expound on these particular types of speeches because we felt they were most relevant in someone's climb to higher levels of speaking opportunities. Choosing the right speech for your circumstances will take a little discernment, which is ultimately a personal decision. We didn't go into detail about every type of speech; we just gave you our starting five. It doesn't mean the others aren't worthy to play in this game.

Here are a few honorable mentions:

- **One on One Stage Interviews**
- **Drama Club Speeches**
- **Theatre**
- **The Poetry Speeches**
- **The Entertaining Speech**

- **The Debate**
- **The Humorous Speech**
- **The Persuasive Speech**
- **The Oratorical Speech**
- **The Special Occasion**
- **The Sales Pitch**
- **The Farewell Speech**
- **The Explanatory Speech**
- **The Eulogy**
- **The Forensic**

2 Timothy 2:15, Kings James Version of the *Bible,* says, "*Study to show thyself approved unto God, a workman that needeth not to be ashamed, rightly dividing the word of truth*." We can simplify that to be your encouragement to look up and study those different types of speeches yourself. You can proudly add them to your repertoire for your unique situations. The money of public speaking

Chapter Twelve:
$tati$tical Pay $alarie$

The Money of Public $peaking. Let's talk compensation: it is certainly the type of talk everyone likes to listen to. We pay our full attention, as we should because the love of the game will only gift us so far. There's no shame in asking for payment. The only hiccup to that is you must think you have value and be confident enough to speak on it. Closed mouths don't get fed, so that's your cue to raise the bar for your compensation. We hope you go into this industry with a mind to be paid. Don't be deceived; you are worth the highest dollar amount that you can negotiate.

The pay scale of different speaking occupations varies. Your personality type may be a match for these professions or may not. Salary ranges are predicated widely on many important factors, including education, certifications, additional skills, and the number of years you have spent in your profession. Also, the factors are tethered to company size, experience, and industry. Indeed, this book was written for the here and now as a resource for you to consider a career in public speaking, but public speaking can wear many faces. We've explained through this book that you're going to need this skill in whatever field of work you choose. It doesn't have to be on a stage, but you're going to find yourself speaking in front of people more often than you think in society. Do yourself a favor and become good at it; even better, get paid for it in some fashion.

Here are just a few professions to consider:

Teachers Public School: $42,844 average starting, $66,745 average salary (Source: http://www.nea.org)

School teachers and educators of all grade levels instruct students in their subject areas, focusing on national curriculum guidelines. School teachers are highly skilled public speakers and they operate in more of an informal setting. Despite being in an environment where student behavior can be distracting, their daily experience with the youth will provide lasting rewards, knowing they're helping to shape the minds of the future. Their public speaking is underrated in so many ways as they plan lessons that address specific skills and ideas. They also present and reinforce learning academic concepts. Teachers have one of the most impactful roles in society and are worth more than their weight in gold. *Noteworthy:* In the Chapter Eight under **Confidence** we mentioned how William Douglas's teacher challenged him to be better by entering a Spelling Bee, then called his mother so she too could reinforce his inner greatness. Now as a man, he has grown to host many annual scholarship Spelling Bees. Because of that moment of encouragement, William's teacher will always hold the title of a motivational speaker to him. If you have a heart for kids, then this type of public speaking is for you.

Sales Representative in the United States: $69,377 starting salary (Source: www.indeed.com)

Salespeople are the lifeblood of the world of commerce. Nothing works or is gained in business without sales. So, there will always be a high demand for quality salespeople. This speaking professional uses their gifts and talents to sell products or services to customers on behalf of a business or company. The needs are identified and then the recommendations are made as they help their customers make an educated purchase.

The salesperson has the hustle and mindset to know that repetition is key to perfection. At the core, this type of public speaker is quick on their feet with witty comebacks to mitigate objections and push through any rejections. The ability to not take a business deal personally and to carry outcomes with short-term memory is what allows them to keep a positive, upbeat persona in front of the next customer. Being an auto salesperson, insurance agent, real estate agent, or even a stock broker are just a few examples where you'll find opportunities as a salesperson.

The fact is, you can't find a service or product being offered where a sale doesn't need to be made. Your only focuses are prospecting, presentations, closings, follow-ups, referrals, and customer satisfaction. You don't need much experience to succeed as a salesperson; just hustle, determination, and a willingness to get better every day. Your gift of gab may be what sets you apart and takes you to the top.

Politician: $102,220 average salary (Source: www.comparably.com)

The most powerful public speaker of today's time is the politician. The role a politician plays is significant in the inner workings of governmental state systems. They campaign for an elected office in order to be in a position to make public policy official. Society has its hang-ups about politicians but the fact is that they are useful when it comes to making the playing field even for common citizens.

The politician is the cream of the crop level to reach in public speaking. A politician's stage is a world stage that ranges from country to country—a true visionary in their own right with plans to uplift their supporting constituents. The person who stands behind these kinds of podiums has to be prepared to thread the eye of a needle when it comes to precise verbiage. Confidence will determine how they move through a room of vultures and come up unscathed.

Politicians get a bad rap, but there is a purpose for the ones who speak for the people and stand for the greater cause. The most monumental mouthpieces have graced the microphone behind the title of a politician. The loudest voice you'll ever hear in the United States of America is the voice of a President who is considered the leader of the free world. Each speech has the power to change a generational stance and could outlast the test of time. A political profession may be for you if you're seeking a highly visible platform and a chance to have your hand in local and statewide governmental affairs. If your fortunate enough to have earned the trust and the ear of the public, hopefully your voice will exude diplomacy.

Spokesperson: $103,920 annually; majority range $75,000-$128,500. (Source: www.ziprecruiter.com)

The spokesperson, one who speaks on behalf of any company or organization, serves as the face and voice of the brand. They communicate the ideas, messages and mission statement to the public and all media outlets. As a spokesperson, the job is only to assure that an honorable narrative surrounds the company, so speaking becomes an art of mastering a poised tongue.

Public relations is your first language as you supervise public conversation about your organization. As the spokesperson and representative, you are charged to uphold the respected image of integrity that is attached to their establishment. If you're drawn to high-profile situations, have thick skin to withstand the critiquing interviewers, and can stomach high-pressure events and press conferences, you'll do great as a spokesperson.

Clergy: $66,000-$130.000 (Source: www.salary.com)

Pastors, preachers, bishops, ministers, reverends, priests, and rabbis are all considered clergy. They are ordained to perform religious tasks such as speaking to a congregation of members who attend church gatherings regularly. The depth of influence granted to this type of public speaking has risen to another level. It invites a person to be involved in a cause by using the informative, inspiring, motivational, and transformative approach, all interchanging at once.

The one who preaches from a spiritual motivation and Godly inspiration has always shown to have a powerful draw. In our experience, such a convicted speaker usually possesses a charismatic vocabulary to get people to follow their lead. These public speakers usually preach to the ones who want to be preached to. They are known for their ability to deliver a heartfelt yet thought-provoking message called sermons. Most of the content in their message is based on their personal experiences, the scriptures in the Bible, as well as other books of faith, along with other historical references and literature.

We're not here to sway your beliefs about this type of speaker or their presentation, but we do know that some of the largest crowds are tuning in to what is being said. All over the world, someone is sitting under the words of these masterful orators. We suggest that if you are called to this profession or to serve as a type of clergy, you take it seriously and don't play with it. Move with the integrity of your message and practice what you preach, and your rewards will be plentiful.

Stand-Up Comedian: $26,480-$281,435, averaging $60,081 depending on location. (Source: www.comparably.com)

Comedians are tasked with one of the most important jobs: making people laugh. They are the ultimate public speakers because they are stewards of people's weekend nightlife entertainment, which is not taken lightly. But there's actually more to it than that because it is said that the best medicine in life is laughter. So, it's actually a great privilege because they are the emotional surgeons people lean on to de-stress their lives.

Doing stand-up comedy, first and foremost, requires very creative writing. In delivering this type of speech, one has to be focused because it's filled with material that must constantly engage the audience while keeping a hilarious disposition. Comics must be prepared to consistently research current topics while keeping up with trends, being witty and controversial, being relatable, and practicing for the perfecting of nuisances in the script. Every performance is like a smooth conversation with the speaker and the crowd.

There is so much opportunity attached to this career selection that we can't cover it all here, but trust us when we say it's worth looking into. What is to be respected above all about the comedians is their courage and confidence to tell jokes under a spotlight and then wait for the emotional response from a sea of spectators to judge the quality of them. Comedy is one of the most fascinating public speaking scenes, and we encourage anyone who has a natural talent for making people laugh to try this path as an option.

Network Marketer

If you decide to look into network marketing, you should know that one of the most important skills to master is how to invite prospects to a presentation. This presentation is where you showcase your products, services, or business opportunities and persuade them to join your team or become your customers. It is unique because experience is not a factor, only confidence. If you're the chosen presenter, you will find yourself speaking on Zoom calls and or in small living rooms, meeting rooms, and on stages of auditoriums all over the world.

Be cautious when exploring marketing companies you may want to join and represent. Big promises of financial freedom are often made in this industry, while concealing the hard work that comes along with it. The three principles that cover a rewarding journey as a network marketer are having a burning desire, a willingness to work, and being humble enough to be coached.

Network marketing professionals are some of the most skilled speakers because the main ideology in this industry is to become a better all-around person through personal development. Becoming well rounded is achieved by the books you read, the videos you watch, the audio you listen to, the people you surround yourself with, and the habits or disciplines you take on that contribute to your daily production goals. Public speaking in network marketing is not the lottery ticket you're hoping to save you, but in time, it can be the mature garden you planted to save yourself.

Performing Artist: $30,307 (Source: www.comparably.com)

People usually don't think of performing artists as public speakers, but that's exactly what they are. There stands a microphone in the hands of a voice master, then insert music and choreography. This combination becomes an electrifying public speaking experience for the spectators. Singers of all genres, like country, rock, soul, R&B, and rap included create a euphoric fantasy for their fans throughout their performances. Their voice has a message that is carried through the songs. The performer is sharing that they have the talent and the courage to put it on display, and this makes them a public speaker. The only difference is they're singing the words that are designed to move the emotions of audiences. Music that plays behind them supports them like a PowerPoint presentation, triggering a multitude of feelings like love, hate, frustration, unity, anger, revenge, romance, inspiration, and even chill vibes.

We like to use the performing artist as an example of unadulterated self-expression because they actually possess the power of the *siren*, calling out to the masses in grand fashion. Proving that whenever you're out in front of a group of people, whether you're speaking or singing your truth it's going to be impressive to them. Just know that public speaking comes in many different forms, and you can be successful as an amateur or professional performing artist. Like with anything in life, you practice and have an unwavering determination. These rates are national averages of salaries found on the websites listed beside them as of the year 2024.

Lawyer: $82,073-$110,678 average salary (Source: www.salary.com)

Every lawyer has his or her day in court, and this, ladies and gentlemen, is their stage—a grand stage, at that. All in the name of justice, the scrupulous approach to all lawful matters at hand is their reasonable service. Few things take precedence over the attorney's will to deliver an iron-clad argument in the interest of their client's case. The most critical lawyering skill is communication, as stated in

"The Articulate Attorney" by Brian K. Johnson and Marsha—a good read for those aspiring to pursue a career in law. It attempts to open your mind up to the world of expressing yourself in the midst of courtroom dynamics.

So, as it stands, the trial lawyer and or litigation attorney will often find themselves having to tap into a different style of public speaking called debating. The fabric of the judicial system is held together by the daily duties of a good attorney who operates with integrity. The job description is quite lengthy for a legal counsel person, such as building and cultivating relationships, preparing a variety of legal documents, and discussing legal cost-effective options while developing strategies for clients are just a peek into their responsibilities.

We all know they make a great living for the value they bring so we encourage you to consider this path. Smart money says that being knowledgeable, attentive, a great negotiator, proactive, and a problem solver will work in all facets to the benefit of your desire to be great in this field.

We all can learn from the words of the keynote speaker for training on the Basis of Fair Housing for Tenants and Landlords, Myra Reid, Attorney at Law: *"There's more than one way to accomplish your goal. If the first way doesn't work, try another. If it's worth accomplishing, it likely won't be easy. But you can do it, no matter how many alternative routes you have to take."*

Honorable Mentions for Public Speaking Careers:

- **College Professor:** $1,112-$155,056 (Source: http://www.bestcolleges.com)

- **Broadcaster:** $54,464, but usually between $41,712-$83,170 (Source: www.salary.com)

- **Actor in commercials, plays, TV, and movies:** $50,952-$75,492 (Source: www.salary.com)

- **Business Coach:** $90,366/$76,196-$110,236 (Source: www.salary.com)

- **Tour Guide:** $18,000-$55,000 average base salary, $60,112 (Sources: www.zippia.com and www.glassdoor.com)

- **Curator:** $72,627 (Source: www.ziprecruiter)

- **Health Educator:** The range typically falls between $52,724 and $66,707 (Source: www.salary.com)

- **Corporate Trainer:** $65,515 and $74,455 (Source: www.ziprecruiter)

- **Fund Raisers in 2022:** Average salary $61,190; lowest 25% $46,930; highest $80,230 (Source: www.moneyusnews.com > careers)

- **Event Host/Hostess:** $34,613-$43,756 (Source: www.talent.com)

- **Orator Professional Speaker:** $50,000-$300,000 per year, or more, if they have a well-established brand and speaking skills (Source: www.thespeakerlab.com)

- **Mediator:** $87,671-$98,344 per year. Calculate the 20-year net Return On Investment (ROI) for US-based colleges. (Source: www.ziprecruiter.com)

- **Public Relations Specialist:** Depending on the industry, earn as low as $38,570 to as high as $126,220, according to the Occupational Outlook Handbook.

- **Speech Writer:** $72,832 (Source: www.ziprecruiter.com)

- **News Anchor:** $68,000 (Source: www.careerexplorer.com) (i.e.. Emmy award-winning journalist Joshua Short's chosen path)

The Art of Storytelling

When we enter a museum, the piece displayed on the very first wall places our attention under arrest and proceeds to usher it to and through hallway after hallway of exhibits. Our attention is still frequently attempting to break free but never does and remains in custody until the very last artistic showcase. The speech you give is like the touring of a museum, offering information that can only be so fascinating, but the story told within it is the art. The facts will tell but the stories will sell is a very important correlation to the science and the art of any craftsmanship. The point is that the story has the power to hold persuasion.

The Art of Storytelling (a reference to the album title of British rapper Slick Rick) is the interwoven adhesive of all forms of the public lecture structure—that's public speaking 101 and a must-know principle to always include stories in your professional talks with people. We are storytellers. It's like it was placed in the fibers of our DNA that we're programmed to love stories; they help us interpret each other.

Even world-renowned speaker Simon Sinek can attest when he says, *"Storytelling is the way knowledge and understanding have been passed down for millennia, since long before the invention of written language. Storytelling is part of what it is to be human. And the best stories share our values and beliefs..."*

The reason you are there in front of the room, at an assembly, or on stage is to sell an idea to someone who could drive it forward. If you think you're not selling, then you're wrong twice. First of all, what's your own personal origin story? Because through it, you are always selling yourself, and you are always selling your message. The people are always buying what you believe in most or don't believe in at all. Stories are your greatest and will always be your ally when public speaking on any level. A story is the transportation method that bypasses a person's conscious reflex to repel good suggestions and goes directly to the person's subconscious, which appeases their receptive self. Stories are like intravenous therapy or IV that delivers the fluids, medication, and nutrients into the main vein. When you're looking to connect with an audience, incorporating stories in your presentation is the number one most necessary constitution.

Just study how rebellious children respond to what is deemed best for them. There's wisdom in overcoming the reasoning of a little child's appetite. If you're clever enough to disguise the healthy factors of a meal with a pleasant flavor, then their tasting senses will betray them. A sprinkle of brown sugar in oatmeal or a few raisins on corn flakes helps the cause, and the child finishes the meal joyfully. Far from misleading anyone into accepting a favorable proposal, it's more like you are using a camouflage approach to guide them until their eyes adjust to the bright light at the end of the tunnel. Even the same spinach we grew up rejecting became pleasing to our palate in adulthood after watching *Popeye the Sailor*.

Deliver a story. *"Sometimes reality is too complex. Stories give it form"*—wise words from Jean Luc Godard. The parables, the fables, the accounts, the dramas, the chronicles, the history, the articles, the narratives, and the tales told all gave power to the mouthpieces they came from. Stories have the capacity to paint a picture in the human mind. Never tell a story without a point; never make a point without a story. Named one of India's 50 most influential people, author, poet, and visionary, Sadhguru captivates millions worldwide, motivating them to experience the highest level of their clarity of perception. Sadhguru simply uses stories.

Most times, it's that simple and all you need. Remember, "The Art" has the power to hold persuasion. Never tell a story without a point; never make a point without a story. And you can Scholar Up to that.

The Motivational Speaker (Source: www.motivationalspeakerz.com)

The motivational speaker is who we're really here to talk about. He is, she is, they are, we are, and yes, even you are or will be the spectacle that major events are centered around—the notable headliner. With broad spectrum appeal, this fantastic communicator is at the top of the pecking order in comparison to their counterparts. Let's just say their liberating pep talks touch all aspects of the "here and now" life to the creation of a lasting mindset that breeds productive actions in people.

Their prominence is equivalent to being one's ascended version, a reference to *Super Saiyan level 6,* a highly coveted posture of power made popular by the universe of anime Dragon Ball Z. The motivational speaker, which lies within all of us, is tasked to fulfill the purpose we find or that finds us first. Leadership is the language we speak fluently, and this is what attracts the lucrative residuals. Hired by businesses, companies, resorts, schools, and communities as a whole to relay the message of growth and refinement in personal and professional areas of life. Personal development, healthy (mental, emotional, physical) lifestyles, cultivating strong family ties and financial wealth, wisdom, and success principles are at the forefront of their addressed topics.

The motivational speaker realizes that the people are only coming to hear them tell the story of how their listeners have already won. Having a grasp on the obvious yet only promoting solutions and the building of foundational institutions. There are levels to this, and when unconscious competence is achieved, then the world can be your oyster.

Go and motivate somebody to be their own version of *"Eye hath not seen, nor ear heard, neither have entered into the heart of man, the things which God hath prepared for them that love Him."* 1 Corinthians 2:9.

You can be a motivational speaker; it's not a call to the profession (which may or may not be for you) but certainly a call to intercession. Be that person. Be that person who is consumed with being a change agent and without question walking in rarified air. Speak now or forever, hold your peace. Your microphone awaits.

Chapter Thirteen:
Marketing With Content Creation

If you finally have the itch to be on stage or have always imagined yourself out front motivating others, then good for you, but you should know that there's an untold element to this. You don't just invite yourself, so who's going to invite you, and why should they? Let's face it: when you're finally feeling ready to step into this public speaking space, you need an opportunity to present yourself. Like the natural flow of life, what's for you will be there for you in due season.

Yet sometimes, the seasons of good things move slowly regardless, and this is even true when you're actively pursuing speaking engagements. We've learned that there may be ways to manipulate and speed up the *'waiting patiently for my turn'* process to life, purpose, and business. Have you ever considered expanding your range of expertise? Remember, this question is coming from a why-to angle, so maybe you should.

Without risking boring yourself, try taking up the study in subjects that will make you a well-rounded person. Relate your way of learning to another way of having fun and have some fun because the reality of it is that it's all a game in the end. Learn what you can and pass it on. Become more interesting by consuming the type of information that's entertaining to the ears but helpful to all in its execution. Offering content of substance will always give you a platform to speak.

Social media influencers create how-to material that their followers would consider to be a treasure. Just think how many of your favorite Youtubers you would travel to listen to in person if you had the chance. You assume that they have information that you don't.

If you get inspired to write a book, then you've just become an author. With the title of an author behind your name, it strengthens your reputation package and makes you more of a credible source in that area of knowledge. You can move in confidence and know that you're an expert in it or a scholar of it. More importantly, though, you will increase your value in the eyes of others when you have the right content to offer.

Sometimes, just being someone who has a coveted skill is enough to attract a circumstance for one to speak to groups of people. People love listening to people they consider to be mentors. But if the opportunity hasn't found you yet, starting your own fire might be the way to go. One thing about fires is that even people rushing by have a tendency to stop whatever they're doing just to watch it burn. Sometimes, whatever is burning doesn't matter as long as it's cooking.

So with that, the writing of a book, the producing of a documentary, music video, online program, or just the fact that the masses know that you've had a unique experience will get them calling you to speak about it. You want a way to create a source of buzz so they can come looking for you. The best way for that to happen is to put out fillers in the marketplace. These fillers are things that shout to the public that you have valuable content to offer, and now is the time that they're going to want to see about it.

If you're in corporate America or any commercial field of industry as far as being an owner or company head, then you should consider this book as a major marketing resource. Our Scholars Speak campaign is designed to help your professionals deliver quality presentations in front of your important clients. We offer workshops to companies who desire to have their sales teams confident in speaking on your business model. We're here to serve as assets through this book and by the provision of

speaking seminars for your employees. We can speak directly to your bottom line for sure.

Chapter Fourteen:
Good Trouble

(Techniques for Troubleshooting)

There will always be obstacles to stop or hinder progression. The sooner you recognize them, the sooner you can overcome them. Public speaking can be challenging because things don't always go in your favor. Some troubling examples are fear, anxiety, lack of preparation, technical issues, stage fright, fear of judgment, and poor body language. To conquer the fear of anything, you must practice over and over again what you hope to achieve.

Anxiety is a natural emotion, but it doesn't have to have the final say. This is actually a great time to think like a disobedient child, talk back to your own anxiety, and disagree with any personal pattern that doesn't invite a calming balance. Not preparing for a task is a form of practicing as well. You're practicing procrastination. As we know, this habit can be the biggest enemy to all success.

To conquer this, you must prime yourself to value your time. In order to value your time, you must know the value of time itself. You must understand that time is the most valuable commodity in our existence—more valuable than money, cars, clothes, and houses. It holds a similar value of health and healthy relationships and it can't be purchased once it's spent. It's not renewable, you can't get it back, and it's not promised to be extended.

Chapter Fifteen:
PROCRASTINATION

When you become lazy, you disrespect those who believe in you. Read that again! There's no room for it here or anywhere near you. If you're not careful or diligent, then it'll set up camp right next to you.

Do you ever tell yourself, *"I'll get it done later?"* This lie has hindered the future of hundreds, if not thousands, of potential history-makers. If there's one thing that shows you have no regard for your own time here on earth, it's the practice of procrastination. If you don't know what this term means, simply put, you're waiting to act on an important task for no good reason.

Why do we put off what needs to be started and finished now? Yes, that's a loaded question. It doesn't just apply to getting active in the public speaking spaces of your life; it applies to activating all spaces. This book aims to cover all things for the making of powerful speakers, but we must touch on all things that make a powerful life. We can't detour from health, happiness, family love, success, prosperity, finance, wisdom, ambition, knowledge, growth, peace, longevity, and legacy. The REAL MONEY of it.

Scholars Speak is a motivational guide first and foremost, so it won't hide from anything that needs to be addressed, especially self-sabotaging. We won't imply we're experts in mental health, but there's been research that stated one remedy for mild depression is showing oneself to be productive. Productivity is possibly suggested to be a tool to fight moments of mild depression. We definitely don't know if this is true or not, but it sounds like the fulfillment of purposeful work could bring us a feeling of accomplishment. Those feel-good moments generate the traces of dopamine we need to continue to go after what we want right now and make a habit of it. Ambition without action becomes anxiety. We really hope you get this.

In his bestselling self-help book *The Slight Edge,* author and maker of millionaires Jeff Olson ushered in a concept known as *'the Art of Completion.'* The Slight Edge theme discussed that simple disciplines that, if implemented enough over time, will enable and unlock massive success. *The Art of Completion* was a perspective he used to reach your subconscious into keeping promises to yourself. First, start your project no matter where you're at in life, and then make sure you never leave it undone—no matter how slow it is or how long it takes.

Completion is a beautiful piece of art. If you never begin what you are tasked to do or delay it, then you'll never witness the satisfaction and freedom of an executed plan. As a speaker stepping into your calling, it's okay to make haste to play the leading role in one's own movie. Take ownership of your reaping season by planting your effort now into becoming better. If a paralyzing fear of criticism is a factor in your procrastination, then use F.O.M.O. to your advantage—the fear of missing out will neutralize the other excuse bred by false evidence appearing real. A quote worthy of being repeated..

Rob Gilbert said, *"It's alright to have butterflies in your stomach; just get them to fly in formation."*

Don't let your excuses be the answer. The bottom line is that falling into the habit of procrastinating is a precursor to failure. It's comparable to committing treason on yourself. Don't do it; avoid it at all costs. If not for your own sake, then avoid it for the sake of others who believe in you and your potential. Scholars Speak is the reconnaissance mission sent to locate the uncover threats of an empowered voice, that you may not recognize because they're too close to home.

Five Fundamentals That Intercept and Prevent Procrastination from Entering Your Terrain

- *Start Now, Set Goals (Short Term/Long Term)*

- *Organize Tasks and Have a To-Do List*

- *Don't get Distracted*

- *Reward Your Progress*

- *Avoid Judging Your Non-Progress*

Chapter Sixteen:
Short-Term, Long-Term

Over the years, many of our students have returned to the fold and shared with us their stories of achievements in speaking. They've credited it to the fact that they were able to look far enough ahead by applying the principles of planning.

In the world of personal development goal setting is a well-known success strategy, and its importance is no different as it is imperative with your public speaking journey. You must know what you're trying to accomplish and when you'd like for it to happen. Setting performance targets is a step that must be taken, and no one else but you can make this decision. Time is precious because it defines and makes definite the terms of a project. That's why attaching deadlines can help you avoid the enemy of procrastination by psyching your own self into taking action. Goal setting is another name for this concept and it is meant to force yourself to begin. We suggest you work backward when attempting to set goals.

Think of it as making a soft promise to yourself while having a one-to-five-year grace period attached to it. For example, you set a personal goal of being able to give a speech as valedictorian of your class while not only addressing all your peers but also your family and friends, the entire student body, and every education administration official at your school this time next year at your graduation. Timelines set for a year or more could be considered a long-term goal. Then, work from that point forward to the present.

Make another promise to yourself, but this one is a little more assertive while having a one-month to three-month grace period. Such an example can be your personal goal of speaking for ten minutes straight to a room of your closest friends without stopping about a subject you're most passionate about. Timelines set for less than a year or so can be considered a short-term goal. Now, to make the short-term goal process even more effective, add as many miniature deadlines in between each attempt to accomplish the results. The deadlines make you serious about keeping the promises you have set for yourself.

Chapter Seventeen:
Underdog Stand Tall

When we, as a mentor group, began to step into our public speaking season, we discovered that we weren't the ones our peers had confidence in and not even close to being everyone's cup of tea. In some instances, we've found out that we had more than a few haters using their influence against us in hopes of slowing down our initiatives. The use of tactics that deter progress was strange to us because all we represent is the uplifting and empowering of the voices of children. It is written "*A prophet is not without honor, but in his own country, and among his own kin, and in his own house.*" It's a hard truth, but it stands to reason why affirmations are the cornerstone of an innermost prized value. Your private self-talk must serve as a rationed canteen of water. You'll need it from time to time to bring you back to life in this barren land.

Sometimes, through unknown circumstances, barriers make the paths you seek difficult, and they can have nothing to do with you at all. Odds may stack against you, but even as a public speaker, you must know that as long as you don't count yourself out, then your victory will be all the more fulfilling because nobody will see it coming. The definition of an *underdog* is said to be a person or competitor thought to have little chance of winning a fight or contest. But the funny thing is that most people are drawn to an underdog's story. The reason is that they feel at one time or another that someone counted them out, and they can relate to how it feels to push back, trying to prove otherwise. It's imperative that in every opportunity you get to express yourself, you must seize it. After all it's in that moment, personal growth matters most, because it's when you are truly letting your light shine. Let them see you speak boldly because talent is the weapon that breaks prejudice.

Chapter Eighteen:
Your Life Is Your Business

Public speaking is a lifestyle, and life is a business; regardless of how we feel, there's no way around it. Throughout the years, while reflecting on every class we've been honored to teach, few lessons have left their mark so profoundly than the Your Life Is Your Business segments. This concept is as simple as the title. Still, when we open the mind up to the similarities of two words, *life* and *business*, the room's attention span becomes more sensitive to it as we all realize that both are parallelled in their guarantees. Countless mixed audiences of adult and youth spectators have listened on as we've explained this crucial comparison time after time.

See, you'll find in almost every crowd that a portion of the people present want to pursue a career that leads them to a high-paying annual income, and the other half are seeking a path to entrepreneurial profits. One mindset is thinking of a J O B, and the other mindset is thinking of business. The truth is, it doesn't matter which you choose because both will be running a business and have been doing so since the age they first become accountable for their decisions. You've probably played with this idea without even knowing it.

If you think about it, we've all been there before, a situation where we're being mettled with, being teased, or eavesdropped on by one or a company of irritating people. Finding ourselves beyond frustrated while reaching our wit's end, enough is enough, and we've heard ourselves say to them, *"Hey, why don't you just mind your own business?"* If life mimics art, then from birth, we're all put into a life-size game of Monopoly. If you've played this game, then you know the rules, but if not, all you need to know is the rules are meant to magnify your ability to acquire value, all while becoming valuable yourself.

In life, there are at least two optional certainties, and they are growth in success or being stagnant in setbacks. In business language, there are two inescapable realities—profit and bankruptcy. A business is an entity that offers and provides goods and services to the marketplace. The world as we know it to be is this said marketplace. The deciding factor of a life or a business being considered successful or profitable is the amount of value it brings to the market. When you see that your life is your business, your decisions will be calculated, and the sooner you can grasp this will determine how much of a competitive edge you hold. There is always going to be someone with equal or better skill, drive, and notoriety than you. You must make sure you conduct your business decisions with the utmost attention to detail. Public speaking aside, if you're a person striving to be, do, and have the things you want.

Here are a few life questions to ask yourself:

Am I investing in myself enough?

YOU ARE WORTH IT. Invest your money into any resources offered by the leading industry professionals. Search out other self-help books, videos, and social media community groups you can tap into that help improve and add value to your business as a speaker. Invest your time and money even if you have to travel to the information. YOU ARE WORTH IT. All around the country, conferences are being held, online courses that offer certifications, and there are training sessions to attend. All are available for the betterment and maximizing of your profit potential.

Am I committing enough hours of daily practice to perfect my craft, product, or service?

You need to devote at least 15-20 minutes a day to rehearsing a speech you're about to perform or have already performed. Commit it to memorization. You'll always have it as a speech you can recite fluently. It can be about anything you're passionate about.

Work with a professional trainer or mentor if you're serious about leveling up. Get them to give you an honest critique of one of your presentations. Have yourself videotaped and then study it, break it down, and deconstruct it. It's not a widely accepted idea, but practice giving a presentation at least 100 times before delivering it for real.

If you are good, your confidence will grow, and you'll never be nervous again. If you have room for improvement, you'll know what you need to work on. Visual or no visual, just memorize it to the last word, with or without a PowerPoint slide show presentation. A continual run through of all your talking points is one of the best things you can ever do to become a better speaker.

The 10,000-hour rule in *Malcolm Gladwell's Outliers* states, "*The key to achieving true expertise in any skill is simply a matter of practicing albeit in the correct way, for at least 10,000 hours.*" So, get to it.

Do I have responsible time management habits?

Robert McCall, a polarizing movie character played by Denzel Washington in the film *The Equalizer,* a walking military weapon, has only one consistent piece of equipment and that's his watch or timepiece. He sets it around 9 seconds for a countdown every time he finds himself in the midst of a conflict. He finishes his quarrels in 8 seconds. You can say that time management is life or death for him. As in 80's classic *Back to the Future,* eccentric inventor Doctor Emmit Brown showed us all how important keeping time was for everything needed to create a better future. The point is that you have no time to waste. We've discussed procrastination and its traps. Get you a calendar. Create a schedule. Map out your goals. Time will only be on your side if you value it and manage it with care.

Who do I surround myself with? Who's on my team?

You are the combined version of the people you associate with the most. Choose your team wisely because their habits become yours.

You'll either influence them, or they'll influence you. Something will give. Surround yourself with success-minded leaders. Their income, on average, will become your income. Their social status, on average, will become your social status. Their habits (rich or poor) will become your habits on average. People lie. Numbers don't. If you're going to play the averages, make sure they're in your favor. Choose your team wisely, or it'll cost you.

Are my relationships deemed as assets or liabilities to me?

Someone in your circle is taking from you, and someone is giving to you. If your team is taking from you, draining you, and depleting your life force, then they are a liability. Drop them. If they are giving to you in the form of an overflow with encouragement, support, building of reputation, financial backing and wise counsel, then they are an asset. Keep them.

John Maynard Keynes: *"Words ought to be a little wild, for they are the assaults of thought on the unthinking."*

Someone who often reflects and looks to take accountability on how to move in this business world called *life* will reap the results of what they plant. The decisions you make today will dictate the outcome of the rest of your life. Make smart decisions, decisions that breed profits like healthy bodies, mental wellness, lots of money, loving family and friendships, meaningful purpose and lasting legacy. A profitable business is a profitable life. Be the example so you can be the successful business owner the upcoming generation can look up to and say, *"That's where I want to be in life."*

Chapter Nineteen:
Call-To-Action

Scholars Speak...   ~The Application~

Now that you have been introduced to the information of the world of public speaking, hopefully, it has given you the motivation you need to know that you can achieve, and now is the time to take action. If you don't know where to begin, then we implore you to just begin anyway. Seek out anyone who speaks at the capacity you hope to one day. A mentor will help most.

If you've learned anything of value from this book, then you can consider it to be an infinite mentor you can lean on at any time. The reach of its content can become even more real because we are officially inviting you into our private community of public speakers. Yes, this is a call to action, and we're lending our hand not only to help educate but to promote and elevate.

If you're serious or curious about this life and career, then what you need to do next is register to enter the Scholars Speak program course. Scholars Speak allows you to experience in real-time the start and finishing of your vocal product. We know that the ideas you carry are like precious cargo, so this course can be thought of as an automatic railway switch because Scholars Speak is designed to be that tunnel tool that places you on the right track.

We've prescribed to the idea that it's not us but it's our students that deserve a platform that catapults them to the front line of the public speaking industry. Scholar Speaks is our program and our speaker's bureau agency that recruits young and aspiring professional speakers. No matter the years of experience, you'll realize the earning potential of the power of conversation as soon as you receive that first check. It's not disingenuous to seek the affluence of it all, but how gratifying would it be to know that someone is seeking out your time, voice, knowledge, and ability to inspire. That's where the Scholars Speak agency comes in to align with you and your passion for expression.

We are looking for you if you're looking for us. We are promoters of your talent and will find you opportunities to showcase your skills and be compensated. Not only will the Scholars Speak agency seek out speaking engagements for its agents, but the program that stems from this book will train and work with our ambassadors to perfect their speeches.

Your age is not a factor when it comes to this opportunity. Only your desire, willingness to work, and level of coachability are evaluated. We are always actively recruiting ages ranging from as young as 8 years old. This book is your first interview, and as we stated previously, only desire, work ethic, and being coachable are the stipulations and the prerequisites of qualification for enrollment.

Scholars Speak is a ledger containing accounts of which debits and credits are posted from the entries of our experience in the field. This collection of precepts were always suggestive chaperones ushering you to start somewhere, while never leaving you out there lost and vulnerable. As we draw to a close, we want to say that there are no moral victories for reading this book. The activity that follows the reading is what the world will be waiting to listen to. American historian Carter G. Wilson wrote *"Philosophers have long conceded, however, that every man has two educators: 'that which is given to him, and the other that which he gives himself. Of the two kinds the latter is by far the more desirable. Indeed all that is most worthy in man he must work out and conquer for himself."* Becoming a fundamentally sound public speaker is our hope for you, so re-examine our foundation chapters 5-10, make a plan then execute, review and adjust, then execute again. Yes, motivation is the standing goal for this book, but from the beginning, we stated more than anything that this was a why-to guide. So, above all, the *why you should* is defined by your level of desire; also, the *why you should* is defined by your hard work, and lastly, the *why you should act now* is expressed by your willingness to be mentored.

To conclude, this book was single-minded in its dedication to the coaches and mentors, so it's only fitting to reiterate the archetype of Dale Carnegie's contribution. In his words from *The Art of Public Speaking* *"Destiny is not a matter of chance. It is a matter of choice. The world owes its progress to the men who have dared. All things are ready if the mind be so."* You can seek asylum in these words. From here on, Scholars Speak is a call to action, the application, we're challenging you to register and enroll at our website: www.gentlemenandscholarsinc.com. Contact us at our email: scholarup1@gmail.com.

It's a detailed step-by-step process that makes you part of our community of young and seasoned professionals. We take you through the many dimensions of developing a monument mouthpiece. **Speak now or forever, hold your peace... shout out and much love to the Scholaring Up nation!**

Acknowledgments

Cory Brazier

As a man of faith, a father, husband, brother, and son, I've been more than blessed to have a village that encourages and builds me up. Despite the hard times, difficult times, and impossible times, there was hope ever present around me through it all. I want to thank my Heavenly Father first and foremost for His provision, His peace, His wisdom, His grace, and mercy over my life; my family (my wife Monica, my daughters Corriana Serene, Moriah Corae' and Divine) for their unwavering support, love and willingness to celebrate me in the midst of my wins as well as my losses. I want to thank my parents, Harold and Margaret Brazier, for their unconditional love and prayers, my sisters Marci Grayson and Myra Reid, and my brothers Ivan Brazier and Michael Brazier for having my back no matter what. To my extended family members, my closest friends, and all loved ones, AAS (alive and shining); they have been invaluable to my life, never judging me. I appreciate you all for being there for me for real, much love to you. To my GAS boys brothers, Will and Shane, I appreciate you both for the wise counsel, and never forget our steps are ordered so let us continue to walk with purpose.

William Douglas

Scholars Speak: A Motivational Guide to A Monumental Mouthpiece is a *"how-to"* conversation of my life and how I may *"give back"* to others on their journey to become the best version of themselves. This is a story of Faith being rewarded, and none of this success story would be possible if not for the people closest to me.

My mother, Gloria, who always encouraged me to let my *"light"* shine! My wife, Rhonda, daughters Rania and Ilana, and my son, William Xavier, who have cheered, laughed, cried, and celebrated each and every endeavor I set out to accomplish. Everything I do, I do with them in mind.

My beautiful sisters, Faniese, Latrice, Tyshaneka & Tyanna, who inspire me to be the best "big brother" I can be, hope I continue to make you proud!

My brothers, Dennis, Brandon, Robert & Tony (We Did It Bros!!!), you are all super talented go-getters in your own right! Thanks for being a consistent example of what *"hustle"* looks like!

Special shoutouts to my uncles, Homer Jr. Joe Willie, James Arthur, Jerry (RIP), and especially Earnest (EJ): The Originators of Gentlemen and Scholars! You have poured into my entire peer group; thank you! Through my ministry, none of your lessons shall go in vain!

Special thank you to Arthur "Butch" Kelley!

My cousin, who's the epitome of a Gentleman and Scholar, your mentorship is invaluable!

My Executive Advisor: Christopher Shawn Thomas, our communication/relationship has no timeline or limits. Appreciate you, brother, for pushing me to be the very best version of myself. My man!

My Circle: Brad Fowler, Andre Anderson & Curtis Bethel. Over 35 years of brotherhood! Thank you for keeping me grounded and valuing our relationship all these years!

My G.A.S Brothers: Cory & Shane! God makes no mistakes. Having you brothers in my life has enhanced my purpose tremendously! We've done so much, with much, much more to accomplish!

Scholar Up!

Most importantly, my Lord and Savior, Jesus Christ! Without Him, none of this would be possible! You've blessed me more than I deserve, and with my every breath, I'll continue to serve your children!

S.R. Williams I

This book would not have been possible without the support, encouragement, and guidance of so many wonderful people.

First and foremost, I want to express my deepest gratitude to the Most High, the lover of my soul, my Heavenly Father. Thank you for the strength, inspiration, and guidance that have carried me through each step of this and all my journeys. Your blessings have been the foundation of my work, and without Your grace, none of this would have been possible.

Nothing I do would have been possible without the love, patience, and support of my family. To my wonderful wife, Cara Williams, thank you for being my partner through every late night and early morning, for believing in me, and for handling so much so that I could focus on bringing this project to life. Your strength and encouragement have been my greatest sources of inspiration, and I am endlessly grateful.

To my children, ReShana, Shane, Jacob, Inez, and Levi, thank you for reminding me to take the time to stop and enjoy the moments and for filling my life with so much laughter and joy. You are my greatest motivation, and I hope this book shows you the importance of pursuing your passions, never giving up, and that your voice is your *'Superpower!'*

I would like to express my heartfelt gratitude to my parents, Late Dr. Wanda I. Williams and Rev. Dr. Sylvester Williams, Jr., whose guidance, wisdom, and unwavering belief in me have been the backbone of my journey. Thank you, Mom, for always encouraging me to do my best regardless of how small or huge the assignment is, and Dad, for your mentorship and for instilling in me the values of hard work and perseverance. Your encouragement has motivated me in ways words cannot fully capture, and I am forever grateful for your support.

I want to give a BIG shoutout to my big brothers, Lamont and Shawn, who have been my role models, mentors, and greatest supporters. Thank you for molding me, guiding me, keeping me grounded, and always showing me the way. Your influence has shaped who I am, and I am beyond grateful for your wisdom, strength, and constant encouragement.

I am deeply grateful to my incredible co-authors, my brothers Cory and William. Working alongside you has been an inspiring and rewarding journey. Thank you for your expertise, creativity, and dedication. Each of you brought unique strengths and perspectives to this project, and this book would not have been possible without our shared efforts and vision. Thank you for your hard work, patience, and the many countless hours spent refining each chapter. I am honored to have had the opportunity to collaborate with such talented individuals; both of y'all are 'The Most!!!'

To ALL my family, friends, and everyone who has cheered me on throughout this journey, thank you for your support and belief in me.

Finally, to every reader who picks up this book, thank you. Your support and curiosity make it all worthwhile. I hope these pages inspire and resonate with you as much as they have with us.

Scholar Up!!!

About The Author

Meet Cory Brazier

The Director of Presentations for Gentlemen and Scholars Inc.—a non-profit co-ed mentorship organization based out of South Bend,

Indiana. Cory is also the co-owner of Brazier-Fit Boxing—the fitness company and School of Boxing that was formed by modeling the techniques and strength regimen of his father, former #1 ranked champion boxer Harold Brazier. Cory was born and raised in South Bend and has a mindset that is well aware of the current pulse of the community. Cory's passions are along the lines of a strong family bond, holistic health and wellness, the finding of one's effortless purpose and financial empowerment. Authoring Scholars Speak has been his very own lifetime achievement award he gets to present to himself. This manuscript documents the depths of Cory's public speaking philosophies that have been a staple for the negotiation of his destiny as one with influence.

Expertise and Experience: Since 2014, Cory has allowed most of his time to be devoted to volunteering and community service as a mentor with Gentlemen and Scholars Inc. He currently teaches kids of all age levels etiquette, life skill concepts, and emotional intelligence, along with teaching boxing classes to the families, teachers, and the youth of his community. Cory was instructed and trained by his father in the art of boxing as a young child. Consequently, he is competent in the demonstration of various boxing styles and proficient in their execution to simplify all skill types. Over the past 16 years, he has gained much of his experience in public speaking by delivering motivational speeches and concerts on various stages, such as in school classrooms, colleges, churches, prisons, parades, theme parks, clubs, recreation centers, spelling bees, and juvenile centers to the youth as a performing artist, mindset mentor, and health coach. Understanding the importance of self-education, purposeful reading, prayer, and mindful meditation are his main obsessions. By applying all the principles of what so many books have taught him (about people, relationships, business, communication, finances, a spiritual life, and health), Cory has accepted the challenge and set out to assist his youth and adult students in accomplishing their peak physical, emotional and intellectual goals. His commitment to daily preparation, smart work, practice, and patience has enabled him to successfully mentor teenagers in building their self-esteem and leadership skills while even counseling his fellow peers in the ways of holistic well-being. Honored as a recipient of the 2021 South Bend Black History Obama Award for outstanding volunteer contributions and community service by the City of South Bend, Indiana; Recipient of the 2022 City Remnant Hidden Hero: Faces of Mentorship Award, Cory serves his community as a health coach, motivator, mentor, events promoter, trainer, organizer, and visionary.

Meet William Douglas

I am an ambassador of mentoring and a champion of children! The core of what drives my belief system begins with strong family ties, community service, and creating substantial relationships to better help serve the youth of the community. Realizing now more than ever in my life that I become what I aspire to be by whole-heartedly living my life through positive affirmations.

A renewed mindset of purpose and service has allowed me growth and awareness of the need to take notice of all the aspects of my life. This passion to create the best version of myself, has turned into my ministry that I believe will benefit all youth. Throughout my adult years, I've volunteered, I've coached, I've mentored many youths from various socio-economic backgrounds in an effort to instill confidence and high self-esteem. The negative hurdles on my track to success that surrounded me could/should have derailed my progress. However, they set me up for spiritual enlightenment, which ultimately introduced me to a path of service, specifically for the youth.

Being energetic about my own personal growth and development, I became a better husband, better father, better brother, and better mentor. I became a student of knowledge, a "PUBLIC SPEAKER," and now, I am a motivator of my peers, the community's youth, and many others.

I am the founder and CEO of a non-profit called Gentlemen and Scholars Inc., where our mission is to empower the youth with the skills necessary to become better versions of themselves. Yes, I am. However, my journey is still flowing in "real-time" as I devote my time to accepting the challenge of assisting the youth and adult community in reaching the physical and intellectual goals that they have deep within. My gift and my mission have become synonymous. I am here to listen, reflect, and encourage youth to step towards their path of self-worth, self-love, and self-confidence in order to help themselves and others! I am currently becoming the "Greatest

Version of Myself," and on my honor… I will continue to help others become theirs!

Notable Accomplishments

- 2020 Martin Luther King Community Service Award Recipient of St Joseph County
- 2022 City Remnant Hidden Hero: Faces of Mentorship Award Recipient
- 2023 Who's Who Global Induction Recipient
- Non-Profit

Meet S. R. Williams I

S. R. Williams I is a passionate entrepreneur, author, music producer, songwriter, actor, storyteller, man of God, and community advocate dedicated to making a meaningful difference in the lives of others. As a broadcast producer at WUBS Radio Station, where he and his family have continued to spread the message of Hope and Love to the thriving city of South Bend, Indiana, for over 30 years! Alongside his many business ventures, Shane is known for his active community involvement, and one of Shane's favorite passions is helping people change the negative narrative in their lives through mentorship to help bring them a more productive and peaceful life.

He serves as Director of Fine Arts with Gentlemen & Scholars Master Mentoring Group, which has positively impacted countless lives. Driven by a commitment to inspire and motivate others and his love for storytelling, Shane's writing focuses on helping you gain the most "Monumental Mouthpiece" in every aspect of Public Speaking in your personal life or in the professional field. With a warm, modern, and engaging style, Shane has tried to bring his unique perspective to this book, sharing valuable lessons from both personal and professional journeys. Shane's goal is for every single reader to get something out of this book that would be valuable and enhance their voyage through life. Shane has won many awards and has countless accolades, but he's most proud of the continued work he gets to do in his city, giving back to the youth through scholarships and mentoring young scholars.

You can find Mr. Shane all over the community. Staying positive and promoting peace and love wherever he goes and to whomever he meets! LOVE YA!

Find WUBS at wubsradio.com and visit gentlemenandscholarsinc.com to connect and learn more about Gentlemen and Scholars and their work.

Sources

Links for icons on Freepik:

- https://www.freepik.com/icon/conference_4470303
- https://www.freepik.com/icon/microphone_8310460
- https://www.freepik.com/icon/message-quote_12471130
- https://www.freepik.com/icon/microphone_16126784
- https://www.freepik.com/icon/bulb_16672998
- https://www.freepik.com/icon/bubble-chat_6036578
- https://www.freepik.com/icon/lectern_5648455
- https://www.freepik.com/icon/message-quote_9821579

Made in the USA
Monee, IL
17 January 2025

c7f5e642-d20f-4b94-b32e-5a075c16a8a1R01